THE WI BOOK OF
MICROWAVE
COOKERY

MARY NORWAK

EBURY
PRESS

ACKNOWLEDGEMENTS

Illustrated by Cooper-West Graphic Design
Edited by Sue Parish
Designed by Cloud 9 and Clare Clements
Cover photography by James Jackson

Published by Ebury Press Ltd.,
National Magazine House,
72 Broadwick Street,
London W1V 2BP

ISBN 0 85223 477 5

First impression 1985

© Copyright 1985 by WI Books Ltd.

Filmset by D. P. Media Limited, Hitchin, Hertfordshire

Reproduced, printed and bound in Great Britain by
Hazell, Watson & Viney Limited,
Member of the BPCC Group,
Aylesbury, Bucks

CONTENTS

INTRODUCTION

The microwave oven is rapidly becoming an indispensable fixture in many kitchens, but it is so different from other pieces of equipment that even experienced cooks can be disappointed by results. When I was learning to use a microwave oven, I simply could not believe the shortness of cooking times, and became so frustrated by indifferent dishes that I wanted to throw away the machine. We are all so used to adding a bit of this and that, leaving things a few minutes longer or using a different ingredient from the one specified that it comes as a shock to learn that there is a method of cooking which is so quick and precise that we have to obey the instructions. At last, I have learned to live with my microwave, and hope that I may help others to do so.

The microwave oven can perform a dozen different useful cookery tasks a day – melting fat, heating a cup of coffee, drying herbs, preparing a delicious pâté or creating a tray of biscuits before the children come home – and at the same time save fuel and dreary washing-up; but it does not have to be a complete substitute for conventional cooking, and it must not enslave the owner. It is the perfect answer for the busy cook, for the person temporarily living alone, or for the student suddenly seized with hunger pangs, and it has the advantage of being completely safe for children and old people to use without danger of burning.

The microwave oven is also a most useful piece of equipment for the freezer owner, not only cooking dishes for the freezer, but also blanching vegetables, thawing raw materials and reheating frozen dishes. In this book therefore I have concentrated on recipes which are suitable for freezing and for reheating, but of course they are just as good for immediate use. However you decide to use them, do be careful to read your manufacturer's booklet very thoroughly and to refer to it from time to time, and perhaps compare recipes. There are so many different microwave ovens now on the market that it is quite impossible to write a book which will suit every individual model, but sensible comparisons with the basic instructions and a little experience will produce first-class results.

The energy in a microwave oven is a type of high frequency radio wave, which is safe and does not damage the cells of food. Microwaves enter the food and cause the water molecules to vibrate at over 2,000 million times a second. This friction generates heat in the food and thus cooks it. The microwaves penetrate from all sides to a depth of 4–5 cm (1½– 2 inches), generating heat on the outside layers of the food which is conducted to the centre. It is important therefore not to overcook food initially as it continues to cook for some minutes after leaving the oven, and this is the reason why many recipes give a 'standing time', so that items like joints of meat or cakes can firm up. As there is no applied surface heat, foods do not brown naturally in the microwave oven and must be made to look more appetizing with a sauce or colourful topping. A browning dish, or a browning element fitted to some cookers, will overcome this slight disadvantage.

Oven controls. It is most important to study manufacturer's instructions before first using a microwave oven, and it is always wise to check a given recipe against these instructions to see if the individual oven should be used in a slightly different way.

Types of microwave oven. The most simple microwave oven is a box with a timing device and starting button. A turntable is useful with even the simplest oven as it saves having to open the door so often to turn the food manually during cooking. Some ovens incorporate a stirrer which ensures that the food cooks evenly.

Ovens may have variable power, which may be simply a 'Cook' power, and 'Defrost' power which is about 30 per cent of full power and may be used for slower cooking, as when preparing a fruit cake. Ovens may have a range of powers, and some have selector buttons for the various types of food being cooked, appropriately labelled.

Some ovens now have shelves so that two or three foods may be cooked together, which is useful if the oven is to be used often for a main dish and accompaniments or pudding. The latest and most expensive ovens combine microwave and conventional cooking and are worth considering if a new kitchen is being equipped.

When choosing a microwave cooker for the first time, try to see a demonstration of various models, but also take the time to assess how much the oven is going to be used. If you are a keen home-baker for instance, you will need a conventional cooker, but will appreciate the short-cuts which can be achieved by melting butter or chocolate in the microwave. A student or single person living in a small space might appreciate a microwave oven instead of a conventional cooker, while the mother of a large family might prefer to bake pies or roast joints in a conventional oven while preparing sauces, vegetables and quick puddings by microwave, or using one to reheat or to defrost food for latecomers.

Cooking times. There are a number of factors which can influence cooking time. The starting temperature of the food is important as, if it is very cold, this can increase the cooking time. A round or rectangular dish will ensure even cooking in the time given.

The most important factor is the quantity and density of the food. As a simple example, a single jacket potato takes 5 minutes, 2 potatoes take 8 minutes, and 3 potatoes take 10 minutes (depending on size). A thin layer of food cooks more satisfactorily than a deep thick lump. It is better to undercook food at first and then give extra short bursts of cooking time until the food is at the required stage.

Time adjustment
Recipes in this book have been tested with a 600-watt output microwave oven and appropriate times are

given. When a recipe tells you to 'microwave' this means set it on High or full power.

- For a 500-watt oven *increase* timing by about 25 seconds for each minute.
- For a 700-watt oven *decrease* timing by about 25 seconds for each minute.
- For a variable control oven adjust to a suitable power level e.g. 'Defrost' or 'Simmer'.

If in any doubt, consult the manufacturer's booklet for a similar process or recipe, and adjust the timing accordingly.

Cooking techniques
A few foods, such as pies, crusty bread, battered dishes, pancakes, meringues and soufflés, will not cook well in the microwave oven. Eggs in their shells should not be cooked or they will explode. Frying is not successful, and many people do not care for 'grilling' or 'roasting' by microwave. However, there are so many dishes which are extremely successful that it is worth taking the trouble to remember the few necessary cooking techniques to make them delicious.

Arranging food. Food should be formed into the neatest possible shape so that the microwaves are absorbed evenly. For this reason, a rolled joint is better than one on the bone; meat should be of an even thickness if sliced or diced; and poultry should be very neatly trussed. Food in a shallow layer will cook better, and a cake or pudding made in a ring mould will cook very evenly.

Food with a skin, such as apples, tomatoes, potatoes or egg yolks, should be pierced before cooking to prevent exploding.

Thicker parts of food should be arranged towards the outside of a dish with the thin ends (such as the tops of chops or ends of poultry legs) towards the centre. Food should be re-arranged from time to time during cooking to ensure even results. Small items such as cakes, apples or potatoes should be arranged in a circle with a space between each so that they cook evenly.

Covering food. Most food cooked in the microwave oven is covered so that steam is trapped and a moist result is produced; this also speeds cooking. Clingfilm is often used but balloons up during cooking and so it should be lightly slit with a knife beforehand. Take care when removing clingfilm from the cooked dish as the hot steam may cause a scald.

Stirring food. Foods with a liquid content such as casseroles, soups and sauces should be stirred occasionally during cooking to distribute heat more evenly. Vegetables and minced meat can also be stirred with advantage. If a turntable is not used, dishes should be turned by hand frequently so that the microwaves enter evenly. Food cooked in an oven with a turntable needs to be turned manually less often.

Standing time. Food continues thawing or cooking by the conduction of heat after preparation in the microwave oven. A period known as 'standing time' is given in many recipes when the food should be left in the cooking dish and covered.

Adding salt. Salt should not be sprinkled directly onto food in the microwave oven as it has a dehydrating and toughening effect, especially on meat and poultry. When cooking vegetables and composite dishes, it is better to season with salt after cooking.

Cooking equipment

No special equipment is needed for cooking in a microwave oven, since a wide range of materials can be used, and it is likely that most suitable items will already be in the kitchen cupboard. A great advantage of the microwave oven is that food can be prepared in a serving dish so that no saucepans need be used and great savings may be made in washing-up time. Food cooked in the microwave does not stick round the edges of dishes, which also helps in the aftermath of a meal.

Materials. Ovenware and ordinary glass, pottery and china may be used. Plastic dishes suitable for a dishwasher are also fine in the microwave oven, except if the food has a high fat or sugar content since these become very hot and can melt plastic. Paper towels, cartons and pulp board containers may be used, but waxed coatings can melt. Melamine containers may char, and it is not wise to use soft polythene containers such as yoghurt or cottage cheese pots as these will melt. Ordinary dinner plates can be used in a microwave and the type of earthenware containers in which pâté is sold are very useful for cooking family-sized quantities of vegetables, meat, etc.

Metal should not be used in the oven as this creates flashes of light and reflects the microwaves so that they will not penetrate the food, but small, smooth pieces of foil may be used. Iron casseroles and metal cake tins must be kept out of the oven, and dishes, plates or cups with decorative metal patterns must also be eliminated. Cook-bags or boil-in bags must not be closed with metal tags.

Container test. If in any doubt about the suitability of a container, it is easy to perform a simple test. Put a glass of cold water in or next to the container and microwave for 1½ minutes. If the container feels cool and the water hot, it is suitable for microwave use. If both feel warm, the container is suitable only for short heating as it is absorbing energy. If the container is warm and the water cool, it is not suitable for microwave use.

Container shapes. A round container is best, as an oval one allows food to cook more quickly at the narrow ends. The heat will spread more evenly if food is placed in large shallow dishes rather than deep ones. Liquids may be placed in a tall container so that the liquid may boil and rise. A straight-sided container allows the microwaves to penetrate more evenly than one with curved sides – soufflé dishes are ideal for most purposes.

Special microwave containers. Those who find they are using the microwave oven a great deal may like to invest in special microwave ware, and there are a number of different types.

1)   Freezer-to-microwave ware is made from a mixture of polythene and polystyrene materials and may be used many times. These cannot be used in conventional ovens, and are not suitable for high-fat or high-sugar content food. They may however be washed in a dishwasher, or used in a pressure cooker.

2)   Ovenboard ware is polyester-coated paperboard which can be used in the microwave oven, in the freezer, and in conventional ovens up to a temperature of 200°C (400°F) mark 6. This ware is useful as a substitute for foil, and it will not crack or shatter or become soggy. Fat is absorbed and the special coating gives a non-stick base. The dishes remain rigid and may be used on a table.

3)   Continuous usage microwave ovenware looks like ceramic, may be used in a conventional oven up to 200°C (400°F) mark 6, is non-flammable, and will not melt or warp. These dishes may be used in the freezer as well as the microwave oven and are dishwasher-proof.

Browning dish. Since food does not brown in the microwave oven, use may be made of a special browning dish. This is ceramic with tin-oxide coating applied to the surface of the base which absorbs microwaves without transmitting them. It is ideal for browning items such as chops, steaks, burgers, fish fingers and oven chips.

Packing for the freezer. Cooked dishes may be prepared in any dishes which will withstand the freezer, but if they are to be reheated by microwave, foil should be avoided. It is most simple to prepare the food in a microwave/freezer container so that no time is wasted in partly thawing food and transferring it to a microwave dish for reheating. There are many useful shapes including loaf dishes, divided meal trays and ring moulds, and they are good for those cooks who want to prepare food in the microwave oven, freeze and then heat again by microwave. These dishes should be overwrapped in a polythene bag for freezing.

Utensils suitable for a microwave oven: browning dish, ceramic jug, microwave ovenware muffin pan, glass bowl.

Thawing, defrosting and reheating

One of the most obvious advantages of the microwave oven is the ability to thaw raw materials or cooked dishes very quickly. While it is obviously not thoughtful housekeeping to rely totally on this method, there can be emergencies when it is necessary to thaw a piece of meat, or even defrost some slices of cake for unexpected visitors.

Thawing from the freezer may be done under ideal conditions in the refrigerator, and this is the ideal method for meat, which can be kept in perfect condition while being thawed. The most usual method of thawing is at room temperature, and this is good for baked goods and puddings. When time is short however, the microwave oven provides a perfect alternative, and is completely safe.

If an oven is not fitted with a 'Defrost' output, check the manufacturer's instructions carefully. The method of thawing is to give short bursts of power to the food, and to then allow it to 'rest' so that the heat generated in the food continues to work slowly to aid thawing. 'Defrost' power is normally 30% of the 'High' setting (on some cookers this may be as low as 10%), and then it is a simple matter to time defrosting correctly, although it is always a good idea to check food regularly during the process to avoid over-heating or the collapse of ingredients such as cream or icing. As the process of defrosting continues, break up items such as sauces or casseroles with a fork from time to time. If defrosting poultry, gradually ease wings and legs away from the body. Drain off any melted ice which collects during the thawing process.

Items which are to be served cold, such as cakes or puddings, should be defrosted only until they are just slightly icy, and then left at room temperature to continue this process – this prevents lukewarm softness which is unappetising. Defrosting instructions are given on many commercially packed frozen foods, but it is wise to check the individual oven manufacturer's instructions when dealing with raw materials or home cooked and frozen foods. Vegetables and thin pieces of fish need not be defrosted before cooking with microwave.

Microwave defrosting timetable

Beef

1.5 kg (3 lb) joint on bone	Defrost 10 mins; stand 20 mins; defrost 5 mins; stand 20 mins.
1.5 kg (3 lb) rolled joint	Defrost 10 mins; stand 20 mins; defrost 5 mins; stand 10 mins.
900 g (2 lb) stewing meat	Defrost 5 mins; stand 10 mins; defrost 2½ mins; stand 5 mins.
900 g (2 lb) grilling meat	Defrost 4 mins; stand 5 mins; defrost 4 mins; stand 10 mins.
225 g (8 oz) mince	Defrost 1½ mins; stand 5 mins; defrost 1½ mins; stand 5 mins.

Lamb

2.25 kg (5 lb) joint on bone	Defrost 10 mins; stand 20 mins; defrost 5 mins; stand 10 mins.
2.25 kg (5 lb) rolled joint	Defrost 10 mins; stand 20 mins; defrost 5 mins; stand 5 mins.
2 × 150 g (5 oz) chops	Defrost 2½ mins; stand 5 mins; defrost 2½ mins; stand 2 mins.
4 × 150 g (5 oz) chops	Defrost 2½ mins; stand 10 mins; defrost 2½ mins; stand 5 mins.

Pork

2.25 kg (5 lb) leg roast	Defrost 10 mins; stand 30 mins; defrost 5 mins; stand 20 mins.
1.5 kg (3 lb) loin roast	Defrost 10 mins; stand 20 mins; defrost 5 mins; stand 10 mins.
2 × 150 g (5 oz) chops	Defrost 2½ mins; stand 5 mins; defrost 2½ mins; stand 2 mins.
4 × 150 g (5 oz) chops	Defrost 5 mins; stand 10 mins; defrost 2½ mins; stand 5 mins.
450 g (1 lb) sausagemeat	Defrost 2½ mins; stand 10 mins; defrost 2½ mins.
4 large sausages	Defrost 1 min; separate and defrost 1 min; stand 2 mins.

Liver
225 g (8 oz)   Defrost 2 mins; stand 5 mins.

Chicken
900 g–1.5 kg   Defrost 10 mins; stand 20 mins;
2–3 lb whole   defrost 5 mins; stand 10 mins.

225 g (8 oz)   Defrost 3 mins; stand 5 mins.
joints

Duck
2 kg (4½ lb)   Defrost 10 mins; stand 30 mins;
whole   defrost 6 mins; stand 15 mins.

Turkey
Allow 8 mins   Cover while defrosting. Turn bird
per 450 g   frequently. After defrosting,
(1 lb)   leave in bowl of cold water for
   30 mins.

Game
900 g–1.5 kg   Defrost 10 mins; stand 20 mins;
(2–3 lb) whole   defrost 5 mins; stand 10 mins.

White fish
450 g (1 lb)   Defrost 5 mins. Cover with
   clingfilm while defrosting.

Oily fish
450 g (1 lb)   Defrost 3 mins. Cover with
   clingfilm during defrosting.

Smoked fish
450 g (1 lb)   Defrost 3 mins. Cover with
   clingfilm while defrosting.

Reheating fresh food and leftovers. Food which is
reheated in a microwave oven can taste as fresh as
when first cooked. It may be useful, for instance, to
reheat a complete casserole which has been in the
refrigerator, and this may be done in a microwave for
a few minutes, inspecting and stirring regularly to
distribute heat. It is important not to microwave for
too long or the dish will overcook and dry up. Always
reheat fresh or leftover food on Low. Items being

reheated should always be covered with clingfilm to prevent drying out.

Times for reheating are very variable, and it is wise to consult the manufacturer's booklet, but experience will soon give the answers to individual needs.

Reheating frozen food. Commercially frozen foods now often have microwaving instructions on packs, and may even be packed in special microwave containers. If a dish is packed in foil, it must be transferred to a suitable container which fits the food neatly so that the outside of food will not spoil while the rest cooks through. Food packed in boil-in-bag packaging may be cooked in that packaging, with a small slit cut in the bag.

Home-frozen food which is planned for microwave reheating is best packed in a microwave/freezer container. If the food has been cooked by conventional means, it is wise to pack it into such a container before freezing. An item like a casserole or pie may be made in an ovenware dish which is then put into a conventional or microwave oven before cooking – and the same container can then go into a conventional oven or microwave for reheating. Flexibility in preparation methods is essential to give maximum convenience when the food is needed. If home-frozen food has been packed in foil, it must be transferred to another dish before heating.

When reheating frozen foods, they may of course be reheated instantly on the High setting. However, it is sometimes more convenient to defrost an item such as a sauce and then reheat by conventional methods with other food. The flavour and texture of cooked dishes seems to be better if they are first defrosted or thawed at room temperature, and then reheated.

Handy hints for the microwave user

Soften butter for cake-making or preparing butter icing, or spreading sandwiches. Put the butter on to a saucer, and microwave on High for a few seconds. Butter will continue to soften when left to stand.

Melt chocolate without dirtying a saucepan or using hot water on Low, allowing 1 minute for 100 g (4 oz). Leave to stand, beating occasionally until the chocolate is soft and smooth. If it starts to set before use, reheat again for a second or two. Leftover chocolate may be left in the bowl for future use and simply microwaved again when needed.

Melt gelatine by placing in a mug with water according to the recipe and microwave for a few seconds. Stir well and it will be well blended and syrupy.

Plump up dried fruit by placing in a bowl with just enough water to cover the bottom of the dish, cover and microwave 3 minutes. Drain and dry before use.

Dry lumpy sugar by putting a piece of bread or an apple in the packet and microwaving on High for a few seconds.

Refresh salted nuts by placing on a dish lined with kitchen paper, microwaving for a few seconds, tipping on to a serving dish and sprinkling with fresh salt.

Dissolve jelly by breaking a 575-ml (1-pint) tablet into pieces and putting it into an ovenware measuring jug. Add 275 ml (½ pint) cold water. Cover and microwave 2 minutes. Stir well and make up the jelly to 575 ml (1 pint).

Prepare chestnuts for stuffings and puddings by slitting each one with a sharp knife and placing on kitchen paper. Microwave, testing the nuts each minute to see when they are cooked and ready to shell. Timing will depend on the number and size of the chestnuts, and they should be prepared in a single layer.

Dry herbs after washing well and patting dry. Spread out a handful on kitchen paper and microwave 2–3 minutes, shaking the paper every 30 seconds, so that the herbs dry evenly. Leave to stand and crumble into jars. The herbs will be full of flavour and a good fresh colour.

Speed yeast doughs by warming the flour and liquid in a microwave oven. Flour may be warmed in the mixing bowl for 1 minute on High. To prove dough, cover the dough in the mixing bowl with clingfilm and microwave on High for 10 seconds. Leave to stand 10 minutes, then microwave 10 seconds. Repeat the process until the dough is sufficiently risen. A mug of water in the oven will improve the dough.

Dry flowers in silica gel, using strongly coloured open flowers. Partly fill a container with silica gel, and put in the flower, stem downwards, and keeping the petals separate. Gently fill the container with more silica gel. Put into the oven with a mug of water. Microwave and then leave until completely cool. Brush off the silica gel with a paint brush. An open rose will take 1½ minutes on High; 3 carnations will take 3 minutes, a daffodil 2 minutes.

Measurements
All spoon measures are level unless stated otherwise.
All eggs are size 2 or 3 unless stated otherwise.
Use either the metric measures or the imperial in the recipes; do not mix them.

American equivalents

	Metric	Imperial	American
Butter, margarine	225 g	8 oz	1 cup
Flour	100 g	4 oz	1 cup
Currants	150 g	5 oz	1 cup
Sugar	200 g	7 oz	1 cup
Syrup	335 g	11½ oz	1 cup

An American pint is 16 fl oz compared with the imperial pint of 20 fl oz. A standard American cup measure is considered to hold 8 fl oz.

FIRST COURSES

Pâtés, soups and other starters can take a long time to cook by conventional methods, but with a microwave these dishes are much easier to prepare.

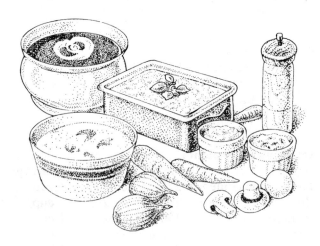

It can be very convenient to use a microwave oven to prepare an appetising first course for a formal meal, because a dish may be made in a container which can be taken directly to table, and the food can also be safely left to cook quickly in the microwave oven without the danger of drying out or burning if service is a little delayed.

Pâté for microwaving should be made to conventional recipes, but may turn out a little wetter than usual because of the speedy cooking. Make a note of this if using a favourite recipe, and adjust it accordingly when next preparing the dish. With the aid of a food processor, large quantities of pâté may be made and quickly cooked by microwave, and the individual dishes may be frozen or stored in the refrigerator under a layer of melted lard or clarified butter.

Soup is easy to make in the microwave, although a great deal of time will not be saved. Stock may be prepared from meat or poultry bones, fish or vegetables. Since less liquid should be used in the microwave oven, this means that concentrated stock may be made, which is useful for freezing, and which may be diluted when soup is prepared. Soup made from tough cuts of meat will not be successful in the microwave oven as the meat will not soften and release its flavours, but otherwise most favourite soups are very good. When making soup with less liquid than for conventional methods, it is wise to keep some stock in reserve which may be quickly heated and added to the finished soup before serving. To shorten cooking time, it is sensible to begin cooking with boiling water or stock which has been heated by conventional means.

STOCK FOR SOUP

Makes 850 ml (1½ pints)

1 set poultry giblets or 1 beef marrow
1 medium onion
1 medium carrot
1 celery stick
sprig of thyme
sprig of parsley
1 bay leaf
4 black peppercorns
850 ml (1½ pints) water

Omit the liver from the giblets (use it for a pâté or an omelette). Put the giblets or marrow bone into a large bowl. Do not peel the onion but cut into quarters and add to the bowl. Chop the carrot and celery roughly and add to the bowl with the herbs and peppercorns. Cover with water. Cover and microwave 30 minutes. Leave to stand for 20 minutes and then strain.

Use to make soup or to add to casseroles. The stock will store in a covered container in the refrigerator for 5 days.

To freeze, cool completely and skim off any fat. Put into a freezer container leaving headspace and then cover. Storage life: 4 months. To serve, reheat and use in soups or casseroles.

LENTIL AND BACON SOUP

Serves 4

100 g (4 oz) lentils
1 medium onion
75 g (3 oz) lean bacon
25 g (1 oz) butter
850 ml (1½ pints) bacon stock
pepper
1 tbsp chopped fresh parsley

Put the lentils into a bowl, cover with cold water and leave to soak overnight. Drain well. Chop the onion and bacon finely and put into a large bowl with the butter. Cover and microwave 4 minutes. Add the stock and microwave 5 minutes. Add the lentils and microwave 15 minutes, stirring twice. Season to taste with pepper and stir in the parsley.

Pour into soup bowls and serve with toasted or fried bread cubes.

To freeze, cool completely, pack into a freezer container leaving headspace, then cover. Storage life: 2 months. Reheat in a double saucepan or microwave 18 minutes.

TOMATO SOUP

Serves 4

450 g (1 lb) ripe tomatoes
1 large onion
50 g (2 oz) mushrooms
25 g (1 oz) butter
juice of ½ lemon
1 tsp dried mixed herbs
2 tbsp tomato purée
575 ml (1 pint) beef or chicken stock
pinch of sugar
salt and pepper
2 tbsp dry sherry (optional)

Tip the tomatoes into boiling water and skin them. Cut in quarters and remove the pips but save the juice. Chop the onion and mushroom finely. Put into a bowl with the butter, cover and microwave 4 minutes. Add the tomatoes and juice with the lemon juice, herbs and tomato purée. Cover and microwave 10 minutes.

Put through a sieve or blend until smooth. Return to the bowl with the stock, sugar, salt and pepper. Microwave 10 minutes. Stir in the sherry if used.

To serve, pour into soup bowls and garnish with fresh chopped parsley, chives, or with toasted or fried bread cubes.

To freeze, cool completely, pack into a freezer container leaving headspace, then cover. Storage life: 2 months. Reheat in a double saucepan or microwave 18 minutes.

CHICKEN LIVER PÂTÉ

Serves 4

225 g (8 oz) chicken livers
75 g (3 oz) fat bacon
1 small onion
15 g (½ oz) butter
2 tsp oil
2 garlic cloves
1 tbsp dry sherry
salt and pepper

Chop the livers, bacon and onion finely. Place in a dish with the butter and oil. Cover and microwave 4 minutes, stirring twice. Put into an electric liquidiser with the chopped garlic and the sherry. Blend until smooth. Season to taste. Put into a serving dish (or 4 individual dishes).

To serve, seal the top of the pâté with a little melted butter.

To freeze, omit the butter topping. Cover the dish with foil or place in a freezer bag. Storage life: 1 month. To serve, thaw at room temperature for 1 hour or Defrost 5 minutes.

CARROT SOUP

Serves 4

450 g (1 lb) carrots
1 medium onion
50 g (2 oz) back bacon
1 large tomato
50 g (2 oz) butter
850 ml (1½ pints) chicken stock
salt and pepper
1 tbsp chopped fresh parsley

Scrape the carrots and chop them finely. Chop the onion and bacon finely and put into a large bowl. Dip the tomato into boiling water and remove the skin. Cut in quarters and remove the pips but save the juice. Add the butter to the bowl, cover and microwave 5 minutes. Add the tomato pieces and microwave 2 minutes. Add the carrots, stock, salt and pepper and microwave 8 minutes.

Put through a sieve or blend until smooth. Return to the bowl and microwave 3 minutes. Stir in the parsley.

Pour into soup bowls and serve with toast or croûtons.

To freeze, cool completely, pack into a freezer container leaving headspace, then cover. Storage life: 2 months. Reheat in a double saucepan or microwave 18 minutes.

MULLIGATAWNY SOUP

Serves 4

1 large onion
1 large carrot
1 eating apple
50 g (2 oz) butter
25 g (1 oz) plain flour
15 g (½ oz) curry powder
850 ml (1½ pints) hot stock
1 tbsp fruit chutney
2 tsp lemon juice
pinch of sugar
salt and pepper

Peel the onion, carrot and apple, and chop them finely. Put into a large bowl with the butter. Cover and microwave 5 minutes. Mix in the flour and curry powder and a little of the stock to make a smooth paste. Add more stock, reserving 275 ml (½ pint). Add the chutney, lemon juice, sugar, salt and pepper. Cover and microwave 8 minutes, stirring twice.

Put through a sieve or blend in an electric liquidiser. Add the remaining stock, cover and microwave 3 minutes.

Garnish with thin slices of lemon, and serve with fingers of hot toast.

To freeze, cool completely and pack in a freezer container, leaving headspace, then cover. Storage life: 2 months. To serve, reheat in a double saucepan or microwave 18 minutes.

PORKER'S PÂTÉ

Serves 4

225 g (8 oz) pig's liver
100 g (4 oz) lean bacon
225 g (8 oz) pork sausagemeat
25 g (1 oz) fresh breadcrumbs
100 g (4 oz) mushrooms
2 tsp tomato chutney
1 garlic clove, crushed
¼ tsp sage
pepper

Mince the liver and bacon or chop them very finely with a food processor. Mix with the sausagemeat and breadcrumbs. Chop the mushrooms finely and add to the mixture with the chutney. Add the garlic clove, sage and pepper. Mix very thoroughly and put into a 700-g (1½-lb) loaf dish or straight-sided round dish. Cover with clingfilm and microwave 15 minutes.

Remove the clingfilm and replace with a piece of foil. Cool under weights. Leave for 24 hours before serving.

Cut in slices and serve with salad or toast and pickled gherkins.

To freeze, wrap in foil or polythene. Storage life: 2 months. To serve, thaw at room temperature for 3 hours.

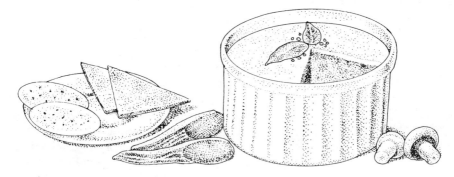

FRESH SALMON PÂTÉ

Serves 4

225 g (8 oz) salmon
2 slices white bread (large loaf),
* 2.5 cm (1 inch) thick*
6 tbsp milk
25 g (1 oz) butter
1 egg yolk
1 tbsp chopped fresh parsley
juice of ½ lemon
salt and pepper

A tail-end of salmon is excellent for this pâté and need not be expensive. Put the salmon into a shallow dish and add 4 tablespoonfuls water. Cover with clingfilm and microwave 3 minutes. Leave to stand for 5 minutes. Drain off the liquid and remove the skin and bones from the fish. Flake the flesh into a bowl. Break the bread into small pieces and mix with the fish. Put the milk and butter into a mug and microwave 1 minute. Pour over the fish mixture and leave to stand for 10 minutes.

Add the egg yolk, parsley, lemon juice, salt and pepper. Beat well with a fork and put into a shallow 15-cm (6-inch) ovenware dish. Cover and microwave 5 minutes. Leave until completely cold.

Garnish with parsley sprigs or thin cucumber slices. Serve with fresh toast or crusty bread.

To freeze, wrap in polythene or foil. Storage life: 2 months. To serve, thaw at room temperature for 3 hours or Defrost 5 minutes.

KIPPER PÂTÉ

Serves 4

175 g (6 oz) frozen kipper fillets
25 g (1 oz) butter
1 garlic clove, crushed
2 tbsp single cream
1 tbsp lemon juice
pepper
50 g (2 oz) unsalted butter

Cut the corner from the bag of kipper fillets to allow steam to escape. Put the bag onto a plate and microwave 5 minutes. Drain the liquid into a bowl and add the butter. Remove the skin from the kipper fillets and flake into the bowl. Add the garlic, cream, lemon juice and pepper. For a coarse pâté, mash well with a fork. For a smooth pâté, blend in an electric liquidiser. Press into a serving dish and chill.

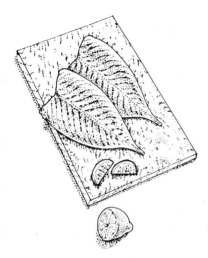

Put the unsalted butter into a small bowl and microwave 1 minute. Leave to stand for 3 minutes and then spoon over the kipper pâté, discarding any milky sediment at the bottom of the bowl. Chill again before serving.

Garnish with lemon slices, a sprig of parsley, or sliced olives, and serve with hot toast.

To freeze, do not cover with melted butter. Cover and freeze. Storage life: 2 months. To serve, thaw at room temperature for 3 hours or Defrost 5 minutes. Cover with melted butter and leave until set firmly before serving.

LIVER AND BACON PÂTÉ

Serves 4

75 g (3 oz) streaky bacon
1 medium onion
1 tsp mixed dried herbs
100 g (4 oz) butter
225 g (8 oz) pig's liver
2 tbsp double cream
1 tbsp brandy
salt and pepper

Chop the bacon and onion finely. Put into a bowl with the herbs and butter. Cover and microwave 4 minutes. Cut the liver into small pieces and add to the bowl. Cover and microwave 5 minutes. Leave to stand for 5 minutes. Stir in the cream, brandy, salt and pepper. Blend in an electric liquidiser until smooth. Place in a serving dish and smooth the top.

To serve, chill and garnish with parsley or thin cucumber slices before serving with toast or crusty bread.

To freeze, cool completely and cover. Storage life: 1 month. To serve, thaw at room temperature for 2 hours or Defrost 5 minutes. Garnish and serve with toast or crusty bread.

POTTED CRAB

Serves 4–6

50 g (2 oz) butter
50 g (2 oz) fresh breadcrumbs
350 g (12 oz) crabmeat
½ tsp black pepper
½ tsp ground mace
pinch of cayenne pepper
pinch of curry powder
juice of ½ lemon
2 tbsp double cream

The crabmeat may be fresh, canned or frozen. Canned crabmeat should be drained; frozen crabmeat should be thawed and drained.

Put the butter into a bowl and microwave 2 minutes. Stir in the breadcrumbs, crabmeat, seasoning, lemon juice and cream. Divide the mixture between 4–6 individual dishes. Microwave 4 minutes.

Place the dishes on plates and serve with hot toast and lemon wedges.

To freeze, do not cook after placing in individual dishes. Cover and freeze. Storage life: 1 month. To serve, Defrost 5 minutes and microwave 4 minutes. Serve with toast and lemon wedges.

SEAFOOD POTS

Serves 4–6

1 smoked mackerel fillet
225 g (8 oz) smoked haddock (or cod) fillet
100 g (4 oz) shelled prawns
275 ml (½ pint) milk
15 g (½ oz) butter
15 g (½ oz) plain flour
40 g (1½ oz) Cheddar cheese
pinch of mustard powder
salt and pepper
25 g (1 oz) Parmesan cheese, grated

Skin the mackerel and break the flesh into small pieces (do not flake as this fish is very soft). Put the haddock or cod fillet into a shallow dish and cover with the milk. Cover and microwave 4 minutes. Drain off the milk and reserve. Skin the fish and break the flesh into chunks. Mix with the mackerel and prawns.

Put the butter into a bowl and microwave 20 seconds. Work in the flour and then the reserved milk. Microwave 3 minutes, stirring twice. Stir in the grated Cheddar cheese and season with mustard, salt and pepper. Mix into the fish and divide between 4–6 individual ovenware dishes. Sprinkle with Parmesan cheese and microwave 2 minutes.

Brown under a hot grill if liked, or

sprinkle with a little paprika. Serve hot with toast and garnish if liked with watercress.

To freeze, do not finish off with Parmesan cheese. Cool completely, cover and freeze. Storage life: 1 month. To serve, Defrost 5 minutes, sprinkle on Parmesan cheese and microwave 2 minutes or brown under a hot grill.

MUSHROOM POTS

Serves 4

350 g (12 oz) mushrooms
2 garlic cloves, crushed
75 g (3 oz) butter
salt and pepper
25 g (1 oz) fresh breadcrumbs
15 g (½ oz) Parmesan cheese, grated

Wipe the mushrooms but do not peel them; slice them thinly. Put the butter in a large bowl, cover and microwave 1 minute. Stir in the mushrooms and garlic. Cover and microwave 5 minutes, stirring twice. Season well. Divide the mushrooms into 4 individual ovenware dishes. Mix the breadcrumbs and cheese and sprinkle onto each dish. Microwave 2 minutes.

Brown under a hot grill if liked. Serve with crusty or wholemeal bread.

To freeze, cool completely, and cover with foil or polythene. Storage life: 1 month. To serve, Defrost 5 minutes and microwave 4 minutes.

FISH, POULTRY AND MEAT

This chapter concentrates on the kind of meat and fish dishes that cook most successfully in a microwave. It includes information on how to roast meat for the best results.

Lean and tender meat and poultry cook well in the microwave, but tougher cuts need the long slow conventional cooking method to give them softness and succulence, by breaking down the fibres. Meat will also not achieve a crisp brown exterior, unless a browning dish is available, or unless the dish can be finished off under a grill. A roasting bag will help to give brownness, or a sauce may be served.

Grilling and frying are not successful microwave techniques and, in any case, little time is saved by using the microwave oven. Boiled dishes such as chicken or bacon joints need long slow cooking and do not benefit from microwave techniques. The most successful dishes are those in which small or thin pieces of meat are cooked in sauces, or those which include minced meat, such as chilli con carne or moussaka. Roasting can be successful although the outside of meat and poultry will not be crisp, but there will be less shrinkage and the flavour is good.

Preparing meat for the microwave oven
Pieces of meat or poultry should not be thick or large. They should be cooked in a single layer, and with the narrow ends (e.g. chops) towards the centre of the dish. This means that the thicker parts of the meat or poultry will receive maximum penetration by microwaves. During cooking, the pieces of meat or poultry should be rearranged and, if a turntable is not used, the position of the dish should be changed by turning so that heat is evenly distributed.

When making a casserole, use a tender cut of meat as fibres do not break down in the same way as they do when cooked by conventional means. Meat should be cut into small pieces, and will be more tender if left to soak or marinate in wine or cider before cooking (a little vinegar in the cooking liquid will also help to tenderise meat).

Roasting

Meat and poultry must be completely defrosted before roasting by microwave oven – this may be done at room temperature or by defrosting by microwave. Before roasting, season the outside of the joint or bird with pepper and a little paprika for colouring, or with microwave seasoning, but do not use salt. Try to have the meat boned and rolled, as an even shape cooks better by microwave. The joint may be stuffed, and this only adds 2 minutes to the total cooking time. If meat is very lean, brush lightly with a little butter; for pork, score the rind finely and brush with a little oil.

Place the meat or poultry in a roasting bag, leaving plenty of air in the bag. Tie the end loosely with string or put on a rubber band but *not* a metal tag. Put the bag on a plate to catch any juices which run out, and roast according to times given below. There are other methods of roasting in the microwave, but the roasting bag gives excellent results and the oven remains clean. After cooking for the correct time, the meat should be left to stand in the bag to finish cooking.

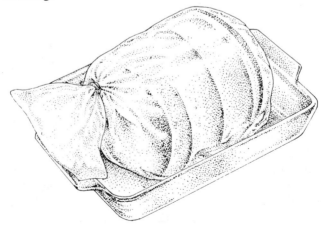

Roasting bag in a
glass dish.

Roasting timetable

Meat	Cooking time* per 450 g (1 lb)	Resting time (total)
Beef (rare)	5 mins	15–20 mins
Beef (medium)	6–7 mins	15–20 mins
Beef (well done)	8–9 mins	15–20 mins
Lamb (medium)	8 mins	25–30 mins
Lamb (well done)	9–10 mins	25–30 mins
Pork	9–10 mins	20–25 mins
Veal	9–10 mins	20–25 mins
Chicken, goose	6–7 mins	15–20 mins
Duck	6–7 mins	10–15 mins
Turkey	6–7 mins	20–25 mins
Game	6–7 mins	10–15 mins

* These times are based on a weight of 1.8 kg (4 lb). For joints or birds up to 900 g (2 lb) add 1–2 minutes per 450 g (1 lb), and allow only half the resting time.

Fish

Fish cooks very well in the microwave, because the quick cooking helps to retain a firm texture. The flavour will be more definite, although some people may find this too strong and off-putting. One great advantage is that the smell of cooking fish is not dispersed all over the kitchen.

Shallow-fried and deep-fried fish cannot be prepared in the microwave, and grilling is not satisfactory. As with meat cookery, the most successful dishes are cooked in a little liquid or in a sauce. Boil-in-bag frozen fish may be cooked very successfully, if a small hole is made in the bag, and there is some liquid in the bag. Other fish needs a little liquid so that it does not dry out, and should be covered with clingfilm during cooking to help retain moisture. Fish should not be salted as the salt absorbs moisture in the oven and causes drying-out.

It is important that the thin parts of fish should not overcook while the rest of the piece is still uncooked. The thinner parts of the fish should be turned towards the centre of the dish. If a number of fillets are being cooked, overlap alternating thick and thin ends, or turn the thin ends under the thick ones so that the thickness is even. Make sure dishes are turned once or twice during cooking if you do not have a turntable.

Timetable for cooking pieces of fish, poultry and meat

Fish steaks, fillets

per 450 g (1 lb)	4 mins on High, turning over fillets and quarter-turning dish 3 times

Chicken pieces (e.g. breast, drumstick)

1 piece	2–3 mins on High, stand 5–10 mins
2 pieces	5–7 mins on High, stand 5–10 mins
3/4 pieces	6–9 mins on High, stand 5–10 mins

Lamb chops	1½ mins on High in a preheated browning dish, then 1½–2 mins on Medium

Pork

1 chop	4–4½ mins on High, stand 2 mins
2 chops	5–5½ mins on High, stand 3–5 mins
3 chops	6–7 mins on High, stand 3–5 mins
4 chops	6½–8 mins on High, stand 3–5 mins
2 sausages	2½ mins on High, turning occasionally
4 sausages	4 mins on High, turning occasionally
2 rashers bacon	2–2½ mins on High, moving 3 times
4 rashers bacon	4–4½ mins on High, moving 3 times

Liver

per 450 g (1 lb)	6–8 mins on High

FISH CRUMBLE

Serves 4

450 g (1 lb) cod or haddock fillet
1 small onion
½ green pepper
50 g (2 oz) butter
25 g (1 oz) plain flour
salt and pepper
grated rind of 1 lemon
milk
50 g (2 oz) fresh brown breadcrumbs
50 g (2 oz) Cheddar cheese

Put the cod or haddock into a shallow dish and just cover with water. Cover with clingfilm and microwave 3 minutes. Leave to stand for 5 minutes and drain off the liquid, keeping it in reserve. Remove the skin and any bones from the fish and break the flesh into chunks.

Chop the onion and pepper finely and put into a shallow casserole with the butter. Microwave 3 minutes. Stir in the flour, salt, pepper and lemon rind. Measure the reserved fish liquid and make up to 275 ml (½ pint) with milk. Stir into the butter mixture. Microwave 2 minutes. Add the fish and adjust the seasoning.

Mix the breadcrumbs and cheese and sprinkle on the surface of the fish mixture. Microwave 4 minutes.

Sprinkle with a little chopped parsley or paprika, and serve with vegetables or salad.

To freeze, cover the fish mixture with breadcrumbs and cheese, but do not microwave. Cover and freeze. Storage life: 1 month. To serve, reheat in a conventional oven at 190°C (375°F) mark 5 for 35 minutes or Defrost 10 minutes and microwave 10 minutes.

KIPPER FLAN

Serves 4

18-cm (7-inch) baked pastry case
225 g (8 oz) kipper fillets
1 small onion
25 g (1 oz) butter
1 tbsp plain flour
150 ml (¼ pint) milk
2 eggs
5 tbsp single cream
salt and pepper

Put the kipper fillets into a bowl and cover with boiling water. Leave for 5 minutes, drain well and remove the skin and bones. Break the kipper into small flakes. Chop the onion finely and put into a bowl with the butter. Cover and microwave 2 minutes.

Work in the flour and then gradually add the milk. Beat the eggs and cream together and work into the mixture. Add the flaked kipper and season to taste. Put into the pastry case. Microwave on Defrost for 15 minutes. Leave to stand for 15 minutes. To serve, use hot with vegetables, or with a side salad.

To freeze, cool completely, pack in a polythene bag or foil and freeze. Storage life: 1 month. To serve, defrost 5 minutes and microwave 5 minutes.

SOUSED MACKEREL OR HERRINGS

Serves 4

4 small mackerel or herrings
1 large onion
4 tbsp oil
4 tbsp white wine vinegar
2 tbsp chopped fresh parsley
salt and pepper

Remove the heads and tails from the fish. Split the mackerel or herrings and remove the back bones. Divide each fish into two fillets and arrange in a shallow ovenware dish. Slice the onion very thinly. Put the oil into a bowl, cover and microwave 1 minute. Add the onion slices, cover and microwave 4 minutes.

Gently break the onion slices into rings and arrange on top of the fish. Pour on the oil and vinegar, sprinkle with parsley and season with salt and pepper. Cover and microwave 6 minutes. Leave to cool.

Arrange on a serving dish and pour over the liquid. Serve cold with crusty bread or wholemeal bread and a green salad.

To freeze, cover with foil or polythene. Storage life: 1 month. To serve, thaw at room temperature for 3 hours or Defrost 5 minutes.

CHICKEN IN CURRY SAUCE

4 chicken joints
1 large onion
1 eating apple
50 g (2 oz) butter
1½ tbsp curry powder
1 tbsp plain flour
275 ml (½ pint) chicken stock
1 tbsp tomato purée
1 tbsp chutney
25 g (1 oz) sultanas
1 tbsp cornflour

Arrange the chicken joints in a shallow ovenware dish with the thin ends of the joints pointing to the centre. Chop the onion finely. Peel and core the apple and chop finely. Put the butter into a bowl and microwave 1 minute. Add the onion and apple, cover and microwave 3 minutes.

Work in the curry powder, flour, hot stock, tomato purée and chutney and stir in the sultanas. Pour over the chicken joints, cover and microwave 10 minutes. Baste the chicken with the sauce, cover and microwave 8 minutes.

Place the chicken joints on a serving dish. Mix the cornflour with 3 tablespoonfuls water and stir into the sauce. Season with salt and pepper if necessary. Microwave 1 minute and pour over the chicken. Serve with boiled rice, chutney and poppadums.

To freeze, cool completely and cover. Storage life: 2 months. To serve, reheat in a conventional oven at 190°C (375°F) mark 5 for 40 minutes or Defrost 10 minutes and microwave 15 minutes.

PARTY CHICKEN IN WINE SAUCE

Serves 4

4 chicken breasts
100 g (4 oz) button mushrooms
½ green pepper
25 g (1 oz) butter
1 tbsp plain flour
salt and pepper
150 ml (¼ pint) chicken stock
150 ml (¼ pint) white wine
2 tbsp dry sherry

Slice the mushrooms thinly. Slice the pepper into 1-cm (½-inch) strips. Place in a shallow dish with butter. Cover and microwave 3 minutes, stirring once. Work in the flour and seasoning and add the chicken stock. Mix well, cover and microwave 2 minutes.

Stir in the wine and arrange the chicken breasts on top. Cover and microwave 8 minutes. Stir in the sherry, cover and leave to stand for 5 minutes.

To serve, add rice, noodles or potatoes, and vegetables or salad.

To freeze, cool completely and cover. Storage life: 2 months. To serve, reheat in a conventional oven at 190°C (375°F) mark 5 for 35 minutes or Defrost 10 minutes and microwave 15 minutes.

DEVILLED CHICKEN

Serves 4

4 chicken breasts
150 ml (¼ pint) natural yoghurt
2 tsp lemon juice
1 garlic clove, crushed
2 tsb curry powder
1 tsp ground ginger
½ tsp ground cinnamon

Use a sharp knife to slash the chicken breasts at 2.5-cm (1-inch) intervals, cutting about 1 cm (½ inch) deep. Mix the yoghurt with the lemon juice, garlic, curry powder, ginger and cinnamon. Use a palette knife to spread the mixture over the chicken breasts, pressing in well. Arrange in a shallow ovenware dish. Cover with clingfilm and leave to stand for 2 hours.

Microwave 5 minutes. Turn over the chicken pieces, spooning over any juices. Cover again and microwave 10 minutes.

Arrange on a bed of boiled rice and serve with mango chutney and a green salad.

To freeze, cool completely and cover.

Storage life: 2 months. To serve, reheat in a conventional oven at 190°C (375°F) mark 5 for 30 minutes or Defrost 5 minutes and microwave 10 minutes.

SHEPHERD'S PIE

Serves 4

1 medium onion
1 tbsp oil
450 g (1 lb) raw minced beef
1 tbsp plain flour
2 tsp tomato purée
1 tsp dried mixed herbs
225 g (8 oz) canned tomatoes
salt and pepper
450 g (1 lb) potatoes
4 tbsp water
25 g (1 oz) butter
2 tbsp milk
25 g (1 oz) Cheddar cheese, grated
2 tsp golden crumbs

Chop the onion finely and put into a pie dish with the oil. Microwave 3 minutes, stirring once. Add the mince and microwave 5 minutes, stirring once. Drain off excess fat. Sprinkle in the flour and mix well. Add the tomato purée, herbs, tomatoes and their juice, salt and pepper, and mix well. Cover and microwave 5 minutes. Leave to stand while preparing the potatoes.

Peel the potatoes and chop roughly. Put into a bowl with the water. Cover and microwave 5 minutes. Drain and mash the potatoes with the butter and milk. Spread over the cooked meat and mark with a fork. Mix together the grated cheese and crumbs and sprinkle on top. Microwave 5 minutes.

To serve: if a brown surface is liked, place under a hot grill for 3 minutes. Serve with vegetables or salad.

To freeze, cool completely and wrap in foil or polythene. Storage life: 2 months. To serve, reheat in a conventional oven at 190°C (375°F) mark 5 for 45 minutes or Defrost 10 minutes and microwave 18 minutes before browning under a hot grill if liked.

CHILLI CON CARNE

Serves 4

1 tbsp oil
1 medium onion
450 g (1 lb) raw minced beef
425 g (15 oz) canned tomatoes
2 tbsp tomato purée
2 garlic cloves, crushed
2 tsp chilli powder
1 tsp sugar
pinch of ground cumin
salt and pepper
200 g (7 oz) canned red kidney beans

Put the oil in a large casserole, cover and microwave 1 minute. Chop the onion finely and stir into the oil. Cover and microwave 1 minute. Add the mince and stir well with a fork to break up the meat. Microwave 2 minutes.

Chop the tomatoes roughly, and add to the meat with the juice from the can. Stir in the tomato purée, crushed garlic, chilli powder, sugar, cumin, salt and pepper. Mix well and microwave 5 minutes. Drain the beans and stir into the meat. Microwave 2 minutes.

Serve with rice or pasta or crusty brown bread, and a green salad.

To freeze: do not add the beans. Cool the meat mixture completely, cover and freeze. Storage life: 2 months. To serve, reheat in a conventional oven at 190°C (375°F) mark 5 for 35 minutes; stir in the beans and cook for a further 15 minutes. Or Defrost 10 minutes and microwave 15 minutes. Stir in the beans and microwave 2 minutes.

BEEF IN BEER

Serves 4

450 g (1 lb) sirloin steak
1 medium onion
100 g (4 oz) button mushrooms
225 g (8 oz) carrots
50 g (2 oz) butter
25 g (1 oz) plain flour
1 tbsp tomato purée
salt and pepper
275 ml (½ pint) beef stock
275 ml (½ pint) brown ale

Cut the steak into 2.5-cm (1-inch) cubes. Chop the onion finely. Slice the button mushrooms and carrots thinly. Put the onion and butter into a casserole, cover and microwave 2 minutes. Stir in the mushrooms and carrots, cover and microwave 2 minutes. Add the meat, stir well and microwave 3 minutes.

Sprinkle in the flour and mix in the tomato purée, salt, pepper, stock and ale. Cover and microwave 25 minutes.

Leave to stand for 15 minutes and serve with potatoes, rice or pasta.

To freeze, cool completely, and cover (or transfer to a freezer container). Storage life: 2 months. To serve, reheat in a conventional oven at 190°C (375°F) mark 5 for 45 minutes or Defrost 10 minutes and microwave 18 minutes.

SUMMER BEEF CASSEROLE

Serves 4

450 g (1 lb) sirloin steak
350 g (12 oz) courgettes
1 red pepper
1 green pepper
100 g (4 oz) mushrooms
6 button onions
1 garlic clove, crushed
25 g (1 oz) butter
150 ml (¼ pint) red wine
2 tbsp tomato purée
275 ml (½ pint) beef stock
thyme, parlsey, bayleaf
salt and pepper

Cut the steak into 2.5-cm (1-inch) cubes. Do not peel the courgettes, but slice them into thin rounds. Cut the peppers into 2.5-cm (1-inch) strips. Cut the mushrooms in half. Put the onion and garlic into a casserole with the butter. Cover and microwave 4 minutes.

Add the steak and stir well. Microwave uncovered for 3 minutes. Add the vegetables and pour on the wine, tomato purée and stock. Add the herbs, salt and pepper, and stir well. Cover and microwave for 25 minutes. Remove the herbs.

Leave to stand for 15 minutes and serve with potatoes or rice.

To freeze, cool completely, and cover (or transfer to a freezer container). Storage life: 2 months. To serve, reheat in a conventional oven at 190°C (375°F) mark 5 for 45 minutes or Defrost 10 minutes and microwave 18 minutes.

MOUSSAKA

Serves 4

2 medium aubergines
1 large onion
4 tomatoes
25 g (1 oz) butter
1 tbsp oil
450 g (1 lb) cooked lamb
3 tbsp stock

Sauce
40 g (1½ oz) butter
40 g (1½ oz) plain flour
425 ml (¾ pint) milk
100 g (4 oz) Cheddar cheese
1 egg
pinch of ground nutmeg
salt and pepper

Do not peel the aubergines but slice them thinly. Arrange in a dish and sprinkle with salt. Leave to stand for 15 minutes and drain off the liquid. Chop the onion finely. Skin the tomatoes and slice them thickly. Put the butter and oil into a dish and microwave 1 minute. Add the onion and aubergines and microwave 5 minutes, stirring twice. Meanwhile mince the lamb or chop finely in a food processor. Add to the onion mixture with the stock. Microwave 3 minutes.

In a jug, microwave the butter for 1 minute. Stir in the flour and work in the milk. Microwave 3 minutes, stirring twice. Grate the cheese and beat into the sauce with the egg. Season well with nutmeg, salt and pepper.

Put half the meat mixture into a deep dish and cover with half the tomato slices. Spread on half the sauce. Repeat the layers. Cover and microwave 10 minutes.

Put under a hot grill for about 3 minutes to brown the top. Serve with a salad.

To freeze, do not put under the grill but leave to cool completely. Cover and freeze. Storage life: 2 months. To serve, uncover and reheat in a conventional oven at 190°C (375°F) mark 5 for 45 minutes or Defrost 10 minutes and microwave 20 minutes before browning under the grill if liked.

MEAT LOAF

Serves 4

450 g (1 lb) minced beef
225 g (8 oz) pork sausagemeat
225 g (8 oz) lean bacon
50 g (2 oz) fresh breadcrumbs
2 eggs
2 tbsp beef stock
1 tbsp tomato ketchup
½ tsp mixed dried herbs
salt and pepper

Cut the bacon into small pieces and mince finely, or chop finely in a food processor. Mix with the minced beef, sausagemeat, breadcrumbs, eggs, stock, tomato ketchup, herbs, salt and pepper. Place in a 900-g (2-lb) loaf dish or casserole. Cover with clingfilm and microwave 16 minutes. Leave to cool under a light weight.

Cut in thick slices and serve with a salad.

To freeze, wrap in foil or polythene. Storage life: 1 month. To serve, thaw at room temperature for 3 hours.

HAM LOAF

Serves 4

350 g (12 oz) cooked ham
1 green pepper
1 small onion
1 egg
40 g (1½ oz) white or brown breadcrumbs
1 tsp chopped fresh parsley
pinch of ground nutmeg
salt and pepper

Mince the ham, pepper and onion coarsely, or chop finely in a food processor. Mix with the eggs, breadcrumbs, parsley, nutmeg, salt and pepper. Press into a greased 450-g (1-lb) loaf dish or casserole. Cover with clingfilm and microwave 12 minutes. Cool in the dish. To serve, slice and serve with salad or in sandwiches.

To freeze, cool completely and turn out. Wrap in foil or polythene and freeze. Storage life: 2 months. To serve, thaw at room temperature for 3 hours and slice.

PORK CHOPS IN ORANGE SAUCE

Serves 4

4 medium pork chops
1 medium onion
1 tbsp oil
275 ml (½ pint) orange juice
1 tbsp wine vinegar
1 tbsp soft light brown sugar
2 tsp cornflour

Trim skin and excess fat from the chops. Chop the onion finely. Put the oil into a bowl, cover and microwave 30 seconds. Add the onion, cover and microwave 3 minutes.

Arrange the chops in a shallow ovenware dish. Sprinkle with the onion. Mix the orange juice, vinegar, sugar and cornflour and pour over the chops. Cover and microwave 12 minutes, turning over the chops halfway through cooking.

Garnish if liked with fresh orange segments or slices. Serve with boiled or mashed potatoes, vegetables or a green salad.

To freeze, cool completely and cover. Storage life: 2 months. To serve, reheat in a conventional oven at 190°C (375°F) mark 5 for 35 minutes or Defrost 5 minutes and microwave 10 minutes.

SWEET AND SOUR PORK

Serves 4

450 g (1 lb) shoulder of pork
1 medium onion
1 green pepper
25 g (1 oz) butter
250 ml (8 fl oz) chicken stock
2 tbsp cider vinegar
2 tsp soy sauce
25 g (1 oz) soft light brown sugar
2 tsp cornflour
225 g (8 oz) canned pineapple
    chunks
salt and pepper

Cut the pork in 1-cm (½-inch) dice. Chop the onion and pepper finely. Put the onion and pepper into a bowl with the butter. Cover and microwave 3 minutes. Add the pork, hot stock, vinegar and soy sauce. Cover and microwave 5 minutes.

Mix the sugar and cornflour. Add the pineapple chunks and their juice. Mix into the meat, stirring well. Cover and microwave 3 minutes. Season with salt and pepper.

To serve, surround with a bed of boiled rice. Serve with a salad or with other Chinese dishes.

To freeze, cool completely and cover.
Storage life: 2 months. To serve, reheat in a
double saucepan or Defrost 10 minutes and
microwave 20 minutes.

ITALIAN VEAL

Serves 4

450 g (1 lb) pie veal
2 medium onions
2 tbsp oil
100 g (4 oz) button mushrooms
25 g (1 oz) plain flour
275 ml (½ pint) chicken stock
150 ml (¼ pint) dry white wine
1 tbsp tomato purée
12 green or black olives, pitted
salt and pepper

Cut the veal into 2.5-cm (1-inch) cubes.
Chop the onions finely. Put the oil into a
bowl, cover and microwave 1 minute. Add
onions, cover and microwave 4 minutes.
Add the veal, stir well, cover, and
microwave 4 minutes. Add the whole
mushrooms; cover and microwave 1
minute.

Work in the flour and gradually add the
stock, wine and tomato purée. Cover and
microwave 25 minutes. Stir in the olives and
season well with salt and pepper; microwave
1 minute.

Put on bed of boiled rice and serve with a
green salad.

To freeze, cool completely and cover.
Storage life: 2 months. To serve, reheat in a
conventional oven at 190°C (375°F) mark 5
for 35 minutes or Defrost 5 minutes and
microwave 18 minutes.

FRENCH LAMB CASSEROLE

Serves 4

1 medium onion
100 g (4 oz) lean bacon
1 garlic clove, crushed
1 medium carrot
100 g (4 oz) button mushrooms
25 g (1 oz) butter
1 tbsp oil
700 g (1½ lb) leg or shoulder of
   lamb
425 g (¾ pint) red wine
1 tbsp tomato purée
1 tbsp plain flour
1 tsp sugar
salt and pepper

Chop the onion and bacon finely. Slice the carrot very thinly and cut the mushrooms into quarters. Put the butter and oil into a casserole and microwave 1 minute. Add the onion, bacon and garlic; cover and microwave 2 minutes.

Cut the lamb into 2.5-cm (1-inch) cubes and stir into the casserole. Mix the wine with the tomato purée, flour, sugar, salt and pepper and pour over the meat. Cover and microwave 25 minutes.

Leave to stand for 15 minutes and serve with potatoes and vegetables, or a green salad.

To freeze, cool completely, and cover (or transfer to a freezer container). Storage life: 2 months. To serve, reheat in a conventional oven at 190°C (375°F) mark 5 for 45 minutes or Defrost 10 minutes and microwave 18 minutes.

SPICED KIDNEYS

Serves 4

8 lamb's kidneys
1 medium onion
50 g (2 oz) lean bacon
25 g (1 oz) butter
100 g (4 oz) button mushrooms
2 tbsp bottled savoury sauce
1 tbsp redcurrant jelly
1 tbsp water
2 tsp cornflour
salt and pepper

Skin the kidneys and cut them in half lengthwise. Remove the cores. Chop the onion and bacon finely. Put the butter into a bowl and microwave 30 seconds. Add onion and bacon, cover and microwave 4 minutes. Add kidneys and quartered mushrooms, cover and microwave 3 minutes. Mix the sauce, jelly, water, cornflour, salt and pepper. Spread over the kidneys and stir well. Cover and microwave 3 minutes.

To serve, arrange on bed of boiled rice or slices of toast and sprinkle with a little chopped fresh parsley.

To freeze, cool completely and cover. Storage life: 2 months. To serve, reheat gently in a double saucepan or Defrost 5 minutes and microwave 3 minutes.

MEAT BALLS IN MUSHROOM SAUCE

Serves 4

450 g (1 lb) raw minced beef
25 g (1 oz) breadcrumbs
1 medium onion
1 egg
2 tsp chopped mixed fresh herbs
salt and pepper

Sauce
40 g (1½ oz) butter
40 g (1½ oz) plain flour
100 g (4 oz) button mushrooms
575 ml (1 pint) beef stock
salt and pepper

Mix together the beef and breadcrumbs. Chop the onion very finely or grate it. Work the onion into the meat with the egg, herbs, salt and pepper. Form into 8 balls and arrange in a shallow dish. Cover and microwave 8 minutes. Drain off excess fat.

Put the butter into a jug and microwave 30 seconds. Stir in the flour. Slice the mushrooms and add to the jug with the stock, salt and pepper. Microwave 4 minutes, stirring twice during cooking. Place the meatballs in a casserole and pour over the sauce. Cover and microwave 3 minutes. Serve with vegetables or a side salad.

To freeze, cool completely. Cover (or transfer to a freezer container) and freeze. Storage life: 2 months. To serve, reheat in a conventional oven at 190°C (375°F) mark 5 for 45 minutes or Defrost 10 minutes and microwave 18 minutes.

RICE AND PASTA

The microwave is a convenient tool when rice and pasta dishes are being prepared, as this chapter explains.

Rice and pasta cook very well in a microwave oven although there is little time-saving, as the microwave method takes only about 2 minutes less than the conventional way of cooking. The advantage is that rice or pasta may be cooked neatly in a serving dish, without danger of boiling over or burning, and that washing-up is saved. While the rice or pasta stands in the dish to finish cooking, a sauce may be heated in the microwave oven. This method of cooking also considerably simplifies and speeds up the preparation of such combined dishes as macaroni cheese, and is a great help in preparing such dishes for the freezer when two or three emergency meals are required.

Cooking rice
If rice is cooked by the absorption method in the microwave oven, it need not be strained and rinsed after cooking. Long-grain rice will hold its shape best. The rice is cooked in boiling water, and it is quickest to boil the quantity required in a kettle before beginning to cook the rice in the microwave oven. Measure the rice, allowing 50 g (2 oz) for a normal portion for each person, which will almost treble when cooked. Allow double the amount of water to rice e.g. for 100 g (4 oz) rice, 225 ml (8 fl oz) water will be needed.

Put the rice into a bowl and add boiling water and a pinch of salt. Cover and microwave 2 minutes. Stir well and cover again. Continue cooking for 10 minutes if using 100 g (4 oz) rice or 14 minutes if using 225 g (8 oz). Stir once or twice during cooking. Leave to stand for about 3 minutes and stir with a fork to separate the grains before using.

Cooking pasta
Use a large bowl for cooking pasta, and allow 575 ml (1 pint) water to 100 g (4 oz) pasta. Pour boiling water over the pasta and add a pinch of salt. Pasta will take about 2 minutes less to cook in the microwave oven than by conventional means, so check the packet instructions and calculate accordingly. Inspect pasta once or twice during cooking as it should be only just tender (or *al dente*) when served. Leave to stand for 5 minutes and drain. Return to the container and add a little butter, and toss well before adding sauce or other ingredients.

SPANISH RICE

Serves 4

225 g (8 oz) long grain rice
2 medium onions
150 g (6 oz) button mushrooms
100 g (4 oz) lean bacon
1 green pepper
225 g (8 oz) tomatoes
3 tbsp oil
salt and pepper

Put the rice into a large bowl. Cover with 575 ml (1 pint) boiling water. Add a pinch of salt. Cover and microwave 2 minutes. Stir well, cover and microwave 13 minutes. Leave to stand 5 minutes and drain off the water.

Chop the onions finely. Chop the mushrooms, bacon and green pepper and mix together. Skin the tomatoes, remove the pips and chop the flesh coarsely. Put the oil into a bowl, cover and microwave 1 minute. Add the onions, cover and microwave 5 minutes.

Stir in the mushroom mixture, cover and microwave 5 minutes. Add the tomatoes, stir well, cover and microwave 3 minutes. Mix with the rice and season well with salt and pepper. Microwave 1 minute.

To serve, use as a vegetable or as a filling for peppers or aubergines.

To freeze, cool completely, and pack in a polythene bag. Storage life: 1 month. To serve, reheat in a double saucepan or Defrost 5 minutes and microwave 5 minutes.

KEDGEREE

Serves 4

225 g (8 oz) long grain rice
350 g (12 oz) smoked haddock fillet
50 g (2 oz) unsalted butter
2 tsp lemon juice
½ tsp curry powder
salt and pepper
1 tbsp chopped fresh parsley
1 hard-boiled egg

Put the rice into a large bowl. Cover with 575 ml (1 pint) boiling water. Add a pinch of salt. Cover and microwave 2 minutes. Stir well, cover and microwave 13 minutes. Leave to stand for 5 minutes and drain off the water. Put the haddock into a shallow dish and just cover with water. Cover with clingfilm and microwave 3 minutes. Leave to stand for 5 minutes and drain off the liquid.

Remove the skin and any bones from the fish and break the flesh into chunks. Mix the fish, rice and butter cut into thin flakes. Add the lemon juice, curry powder, salt, pepper and parsley. Cover and microwave 1 minute.

To serve, chop the hard-boiled egg finely and fold into the mixture.

To freeze, do not add the egg; pack into a freezer container. Storage life: 1 month. To serve, reheat gently in a double saucepan and add the chopped egg and a little extra butter or Defrost 5 minutes and microwave 6 minutes before adding the egg and butter.

MACARONI CHEESE

Serves 4

100 g (4 oz) short cut macaroni
575 ml (1 pint) boiling water
salt
50 g (2 oz) streaky bacon
1 small onion
40 g (1½ oz) butter
40 g (1½ oz) plain flour
575 ml (1 pint) milk
pinch of pepper
pinch of mustard powder
100 g (4 oz) Cheddar cheese, grated
25 g (1 oz) Parmesan cheese, grated

Put the macaroni into an oven/freezer dish.
Add the boiling water and a pinch of salt
and stir well. Microwave 5 minutes.
Remove fron the oven and cover with a
piece of foil. Leave to stand while
continuing the preparation of the other
ingredients.

Chop the bacon and onion finely and put
into a large bowl with the butter.
Microwave 1 minute. Work in the flour,
salt, pepper and mustard. Work in the
milk. Microwave 4 minutes, stirring twice.

Drain the macaroni, and return to the
dish. Stir in the hot sauce. Stir the cheese
into the mixture.

To serve, put under a hot grill for 3–5
minutes to brown the top.

To freeze, cool completely and cover.
Storage life: 2 months. To serve, reheat in a
conventional oven at 190°C (375°F) mark 5
for 45 minutes or Defrost 10 minutes and
microwave 12 minutes before browning
under a grill if liked.

CANNELLONI IN TOMATO SAUCE

Serves 4

8 tubes cannelloni
1 small onion
½ green pepper
100 g (4 oz) button mushrooms
225 g (8 oz) chicken livers
100 g (4 oz) lean bacon
50 g (2 oz) butter
1 recipe fresh tomato sauce
    (see page 78)
25 g (1 oz) Parmesan cheese, grated

Put the cannelloni in a shallow ovenware
dish and cover with 575 ml (1 pint) boiling
water. Add a pinch of salt. Cover and
microwave 10 minutes. Drain very well.
Chop the onion and pepper very finely and
mix together. Chop the mushrooms, liver
and bacon finely and mix together. Put the
butter into a bowl, cover and microwave 1
minute. Add the onion and pepper, cover
and microwave 5 minutes.

Add the mushroom and liver mixture,

stir well, cover and microwave 5 minutes. Add 6 tablespoonfuls fresh tomato sauce to bind the mixture and use it to fill the cannelloni tubes. Arrange in a shallow ovenware dish. Pour over the remaining sauce. Cover and microwave 3 minutes. Sprinkle with cheese and microwave 1 minute.

Brown under a hot grill if liked.

To freeze, omit the cheese topping. Cool completely and cover. Storage life: 1 month. To serve, sprinkle with Parmesan cheese, reheat in a conventional oven at 190°C (375°F) mark 5 for 35 minutes or Defrost 5 minutes, sprinkle with Parmesan cheese and microwave 10 minutes.

PASTA MEAT LOAF

Serves 4

75 g (3 oz) pasta shapes or short cut
    macaroni
575 ml (1 pint) boiling water
pinch of salt
225 g (8 oz) cooked beef or lamb
1 medium onion
75 g (3 oz) Cheddar cheese
1 tsp chopped mixed fresh herbs
seasoning
2 eggs

Put the pasta shapes or macaroni into a bowl. Add the boiling water and salt and stir well. Microwave 5 minutes. Cover with a piece of foil and leave to stand while preparing the other ingredients.

Mince the meat and onion together or chop finely in a food processor. Mix with the cheese, herbs, salt, pepper and eggs and stir in the cooked pasta. Put into a greased 450-g (1-lb) loaf dish or casserole. Cover with clingfilm, and microwave 12 minutes. Serve hot with tomato sauce (see page 78).

To freeze, cool completely, turn out and wrap in foil or polythene and freeze. Storage life: 1 month. To serve, return to the dish and Defrost 10 minutes, then microwave 5 minutes.

LASAGNE

Serves 4

9 pieces lasagne
1 recipe quantity spaghetti sauce (see page 79)
1 recipe quantity cheese sauce (see page 76)
25 g (1 oz) Parmesan cheese, grated

Put 1.2 litres (2 pints) boiling water into a large bowl and add a pinch of salt. Slide in the lasagne. Cover and microwave 5 minutes. Leave to stand for 5 minutes and drain well.

Put 3 pieces of lasagne in a single layer in a rectangular ovenware dish and top with one-third of the spaghetti sauce and then one-third of the cheese sauce. Repeat the layers twice, finishing with cheese sauce. Sprinkle with cheese and microwave 8 minutes.

To serve, brown under a hot grill if liked, or sprinkle with a little paprika.

To freeze, do not sprinkle with cheese, but complete the cooking as for immediate service. Cool completely, wrap in foil or polythene and freeze. Storage life: 1 month. To serve, sprinkle with Parmesan cheese, reheat in a conventional oven at 190°C (375°F) mark 5 for 35 minutes or Defrost 5 minutes, sprinkle with Parmesan cheese and microwave 10 minutes.

GNOCCHI

Serves 4

1 medium onion
1 bay leaf
575 ml (1 pint) milk
5 tbsp fine semolina
salt and pepper
40 g (1½ oz) Cheddar cheese, grated
25 g (1 oz) butter
1 tsp French mustard

Slice the onion thinly and put into a large jug with the bay leaf and milk. Microwave 4 minutes. Leave to stand for 10 minutes. Remove and discard the onion and bay leaf. Mix the semolina and milk in a bowl and season well. Cover and microwave 4 minutes.

Stir in the cheese, butter and mustard and spread the mixture on a board or dish about 2.5 cm (1 inch) thick. Leave until cold and set and cut into 5-cm (2-inch)

Topping
50 g (2 oz) butter
50 g (2 oz) Cheddar cheese, grated

squares. Arrange the squares in overlapping rows in a rectangular dish. Microwave the butter 1 minute. Brush all over the squares with butter and sprinkle with cheese. Cover with clingfilm and microwave 5 minutes. To serve, put under a hot grill to become golden and crisp. Serve with salad.

To freeze, do not put under the grill. Leave until cold, then cover with foil or polythene, and freeze. Storage life: 1 month. To serve, Defrost 10 minutes and put under a hot grill until golden and crisp. Serve with salad.

CHICKEN RISOTTO

Serves 4

50 g (2 oz) butter
1 large onion
1 green pepper
1 celery stick
225 g (8 oz) long grain rice
575 ml (1 pint) chicken stock
25 g (1 oz) seedless raisins
225 g (8 oz) cooked chicken
salt and pepper

Cooked turkey or duck may be used instead of chicken, with the appropriate stock. Put the butter into a casserole, cover and microwave 1 minute. Chop the onion finely and slice the pepper and celery thinly. Add to the butter, cover and microwave 2 minutes. Stir in the rice and pour in the boiling stock. Cover and microwave 2 minutes. Add the raisins and stir well. Cover and microwave 15 minutes.
    Chop the chicken finely and stir into the rice. Do not cover and microwave 2 minutes. Season to taste, cover and leave to stand 10 minutes.

To freeze, cool completely and pack into a polythene bag for freezing. Storage life: 1 month. To serve, reheat in a double saucepan, adding more stock if liked or put into a casserole and Defrost 5 minutes, then microwave 10 minutes, stir twice.

MINCE AND RICE BAKE

Serves 4

100 g (4 oz) raw minced beef
1 small onion, finely chopped
1 clove garlic, crushed
100 g (4 oz) red lentils
1 small green pepper, finely chopped
425 g (15 oz) canned tomatoes
1 bay leaf
575 ml (1 pint) beef stock
pinch of dried basil
pinch of dried marjoram
2 tbsp tomato ketchup
salt and pepper
100 g (4 oz) long grain rice
50 g (2 oz) Cheddar cheese, grated

Put the meat into a bowl with the onion and garlic. Cover and microwave 4 minutes. Drain off excess fat. Stir in the lentils, green pepper, tomatoes and their juice, bay leaf, half the stock, herbs, tomato ketchup and seasoning. Cover and microwave 12 minutes. Discard the bay leaf. Cover the bowl with foil and leave to stand while preparing the rice.

Put the rice into a bowl with the remaining stock (boiling) and a pinch of salt. Cover and microwave 2 minutes. Stir well, cover and microwave 12 minutes. Arrange layers of the mince mixture and rice in a casserole, finishing with a mince layer. Cover and microwave 5 minutes. Sprinkle with cheese and brown under a hot grill. Serve at once with salad.

To freeze, arrange the layers of mince and rice but do not microwave or sprinkle with cheese. Cool completely, cover and freeze. Storage life: 1 month. To serve, defrost 10 minutes and microwave 15 minutes. Sprinkle with cheese and brown under a hot grill.

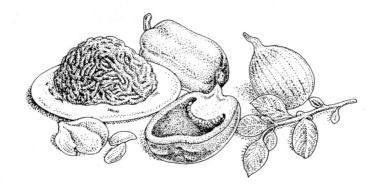

CHICKEN TETRAZZINI

Serves 4

225 g (8 oz) spaghetti
450 g (1 lb) cooked chicken
225 g (8 oz) button mushrooms
50 g (2 oz) butter
25 g (1 oz) plain flour
275 ml (½ pint) chicken stock
150 ml (¼ pint) creamy milk
pinch of ground nutmeg
salt and pepper
2 tbsp dry sherry
40 g (1½ oz) Cheddar cheese, grated
25 g (1 oz) Parmesan cheese, grated

Put the spaghetti into a deep bowl and pour on 575 ml (1 pint) boiling water. Add a pinch of salt. Cover with clingfilm and microwave 8 minutes. Drain very well. Cut the chicken into thin strips. Slice the mushrooms thinly. Put into a bowl with half the butter, cover and microwave 5 minutes.

Put the remaining butter into a jug and microwave 30 seconds. Work in the flour and gradually add the stock and milk. Microwave 4 minutes, stirring twice. Season with nutmeg, salt, pepper and sherry, and stir in the Cheddar cheese.

Use half the sauce to mix with the spaghetti and mushrooms and arrange in a border round a circular or square ovenware dish. Mix the chicken into the remaining sauce and place in the centre of the spaghetti. Sprinkle the chicken with Parmesan cheese. Microwave 5 minutes.

Brown under a hot grill if liked. Serve with a green salad.

To freeze, omit the cheese topping. Cool completely and cover. Storage life: 1 month. To serve, sprinkle with Parmesan cheese and reheat in a conventional oven at 190°C (375°F) mark 5 for 35 minutes or Defrost 5 minutes, sprinkle with Parmesan cheese and microwave 10 minutes.

VEGETABLES

Vegetables cooked in a microwave are richly
flavoured, brightly coloured and full of
nutrients, because they require little water.

Vegetables for microwaving should be young and fresh and of high quality. No more than 450 g (1 lb) vegetables should be cooked at one time, with the addition of 2–4 tablespoonfuls of water. Salt should not be added as this causes dehydration in the microwave oven, but seasoning and butter may be tossed with the vegetables after cooking. Vegetables may be prepared in a serving dish, but must be covered with clingfilm which has been slit slightly to allow steam to escape. Vegetables may be cooked in a roasting bag tied loosely with string if this is more convenient. To ensure even cooking, vegetables should be stirred once during cooking, and they should be left to stand for 3–4 minutes after microwaving to complete the cooking.

Fresh vegetable timetable

Vegetable	*Cooking time per 450 g (1 lb)*
Asparagus	
Broad beans	
French beans	
Runner beans	
Beetroot	
Carrots (thin slices)	5–7 minutes
Cauliflower florets	
Courgettes (thin slices)	
Leeks (5-cm/2-inch slices)	
Potatoes, old (sliced)	
Potatoes, new (whole)	
Spinach	
Artichokes, globe (2)	
Broccoli (thin sprigs)	7–9 minutes
Brussels sprouts	
Cabbage (finely shredded)	

Celery (diced)	
Corn-on-the-cob (4 small)	7–9 minutes
Marrow (diced)	
Onions (sliced or diced)	
Peas	
Spring greens	
Parsnips (diced)	
Swedes (diced)	9–10 minutes
Turnips (diced)	
Mushrooms (225 g/8 oz small	4–5 minutes
whole, not with water, but	
with 25 g/1 oz butter)	

Frozen vegetables
Home-frozen and commercially frozen vegetables
may be successfully cooked in the microwave oven
since they are generally very young and tender when
frozen. They may be cooked in the bag in which they
have been prepared at home, but should be loosely
tied with string or a rubber band (manufacturers'
bags should not be used because of the colouring or
possible metal content of the bags). Otherwise, the
vegetables should be spread in a single layer in a
container with 1–2 tablespoonfuls water, and
covered with clingfilm, slightly slit. Large irregular
vegetables such as broccoli should be arranged with
the thickest parts facing outwards in the dish. If
vegetables are in a solid block, break up the block
halfway through cooking. All frozen vegetables will
take approximately 10 minutes to cook (450 g/1 lb)
in the microwave oven.

Blanching vegetables for freezing
There are two ways of blanching vegetables in the
microwave oven which both save considerable time.

Vegetables should be prepared as for table use.

Method 1: put 450 g (1 lb) vegetables into a casserole with 4 tablespoonfuls water. Microwave 2 minutes, stir well and microwave 1 minute. Drain, plunge into ice-cold water, dry and pack.

Method 2: pack each 450 g (1 lb) vegetables into boil-in-bags and tie loosely with string. Place on a plate in the microwave oven and microwave for *half* the time given in the chart below. Turn over the bag and microwave for the remaining time. Put the bag into ice-cold water, keeping it below the surface. Dry the bag and freeze.

Vegetables	*Blanching time*
Artichokes (2 whole)	3½ minutes
Corn-on-the-cob (4 small)	5 minutes
Carrots (small whole or thin slices)	2½ minutes
Asparagus; Brussels sprouts; broccoli (thin sprigs); cauliflower florets	2 minutes
French beans; broad beans; root vegetables (diced)	1½ minutes
Runner beans; cabbage (shredded); leeks (sliced); spinach; peas	1 minute

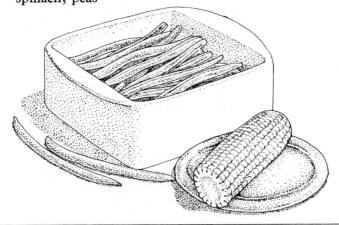

RED CABBAGE CASSEROLE

Serves 4

450 g (1 lb) red cabbage
1 medium onion
1 eating apple
25 g (1 oz) butter
150 ml (¼ pint) dry cider
2 tbsp cider vinegar
2 tbsp apple jelly
1 tsp ground mixed spice
salt and pepper

Shred the cabbage finely. Chop the onion finely. Peel and chop the apple finely. Put the butter into a casserole and add the onion and apple. Cover and microwave 3 minutes. Stir in the cabbage, cider, vinegar, apple jelly, spice, salt and pepper. Cover and microwave 9 minutes, stirring twice.

To serve, use as a hot vegetable, or as a cold salad. This is particularly good with pork or game.

To freeze, cool completely and cover. Storage life: 2 months. To serve, heat gently in a double saucepan or Defrost 10 minutes and microwave 5 minutes.

STUFFED AUBERGINES

Serves 4

2 small aubergines
40 g (1½ oz) fresh breadcrumbs
50 g (2 oz) cooked ham
1 tsp grated onion
25 g (1 oz) button mushrooms
1 garlic clove, crushed
1 tsp chopped fresh parsley
½ tsp grated lemon rind
1 egg
salt and pepper

Do not peel the aubergines. Cut them in half lengthwise and scoop out the seeds. Sprinkle with salt and place cut side down on a plate for 1 hour. Drain off the liquid and rinse the aubergines in fresh water. Arrange them cut side up in a shallow dish. Cover and microwave 5 minutes.

Mix the breadcrumbs with the finely chopped ham and onion. Chop the mushrooms finely. Mix into the ham with the garlic, parsley, lemon rind, egg and salt and pepper. Fill the aubergines. Cover and microwave 10 minutes.

Serve with tomato sauce (see page 78).

To freeze, cool completely and cover. Storage life: 1 month. To serve, reheat in a conventional oven at 190°C (375°F) mark 5 for 30 minutes or Defrost 5 minutes and microwave 10 minutes.

BRAISED CELERY

Serves 4

2 celery heads
8 tbsp beef stock
1 tsp mixed dried herbs
25 g (1 oz) fresh breadcrumbs
25 g (1 oz) butter
salt and pepper

Trim the tops off the celery, leaving the celery bases 15 cm (6 inches) long. Split the bases into quarters. Wash very thoroughly. Arrange in a single layer in a shallow ovenware container. Pour on the stock. Cover and microwave 12 minutes.

Mix the herbs with the breadcrumbs. Season the celery with salt and pepper and sprinkle on the crumbs. Cut the butter into thin flakes and dot over the crumbs. Microwave 5 minutes.

To freeze, cool completely and cover. Storage life: 2 months. To serve, reheat in a conventional oven at 190°C (375°F) mark 5 for 30 minutes or Defrost 5 minutes and microwave 10 minutes.

COURGETTE BAKE

Serves 4

450 g (1 lb) courgettes
1 large onion
2 tbsp oil
225 g (8 oz) tomatoes
1 garlic clove, crushed
1 tbsp chopped fresh parsley
pinch of marjoram or basil
salt and pepper

Do not peel the courgettes but slice them thinly. Chop the onion finely. Put the oil into a bowl and microwave 1 minute. Add the onion, cover and microwave 5 minutes. Add the courgettes, cover and microwave 3 minutes. Skin the tomatoes and remove the seeds. Chop the flesh coarsely and mix with the courgettes.

Add the garlic, parsley and marjoram or basil and stir well. Cover and microwave 6 minutes. Season well with salt and pepper.

To serve, use as a hot accompaniment to meat, poultry or fish.

To freeze, cool and cover with foil or polythene. Storage life: 2 months. To serve, reheat very gently in a saucepan or Defrost 5 minutes and microwave 5 minutes.

CABBAGE ROLL-UPS

Serves 4

8 large cabbage leaves
1 small onion
25 g (1 oz) butter
350 g (12 oz) raw minced beef
50 g (2 oz) cooked long grain rice
1 tsp dried mixed herbs
6 tbsp beef stock
1 recipe quantity fresh tomato sauce
   (see page 78)

Put the cabbage leaves into a pan of boiling water and boil for 2 minutes. Drain well. Chop the onion finely. Put the butter into a large bowl and microwave 30 seconds. Add the onion, cover and microwave 3 minutes. Add the beef, rice, herbs and stock and stir well to break up the meat. Cover and microwave 8 minutes.

Divide the meat mixture between the cabbage leaves. Fold in the base of each leaf, then the sides, and roll carefully to make neat parcels. Arrange in a single layer in a shallow ovenware dish.

Prepare the tomato sauce and pour the hot sauce over the cabbage parcels. Cover and microwave 5 minutes.

Sprinkle with a little chopped parsley and serve with rice or potatoes.

To freeze, cool completely and cover. Storage life: 2 months. To serve, reheat in a conventional oven at 190°C (375°F) mark 5 for 35 minutes or Defrost 5 minutes and microwave 10 minutes.

TOMATO AND ONION CASSEROLE

Serves 4

225 g (8 oz) onions
450 g (1 lb) tomatoes
½ tsp dried basil
salt and pepper
75 g (3 oz) fresh breadcrumbs
75 g (3 oz) Cheddar cheese
25 g (1 oz) butter

Chop the onions finely and put into a deep casserole. Just cover with water, cover and microwave 7 minutes. Drain well and season with basil, salt and pepper. Skin the tomatoes and cut into thin slices. Mix the breadcrumbs and grated cheese together.

Put half the onions in a shallow ovenware dish. Cover with half the tomatoes and half the crumb mixture. Repeat the layers. Put the butter in a small bowl and microwave 30 seconds. Pour over the breadcrumbs. Cover

with clingfilm and microwave 15 minutes.
To serve, brown under a hot grill if liked.
Serve as an accompaniment to meat, poultry
or fish, or as a vegetarian dish.

To freeze, cool completely and cover.
Storage life: 1 month. To serve, reheat in a
conventional oven at 190°C (375°F) mark 5
for 35 minutes or Defrost and microwave 10
minutes before browning under a grill.

STUFFED GREEN PEPPERS

Serves 4

2 large green peppers
1 small onion
25 g (1 oz) butter
225 g (8 oz) cooked beef, lamb or
    pork
75 g (3 oz) cooked long grain rice
2 tbsp beef stock or water
2 tsp tomato purée
2 tsp chopped fresh parsley
1 tsp chopped fresh marjoram
salt and pepper
25 g (1 oz) fresh breadcrumbs

Remove the stems from peppers and cut the
peppers in half downwards from the stem to
provide four 'cases'. Remove the seeds.
Arrange the peppers in a shallow ovenware
dish. Chop the onion finely and put into a
small bowl with the butter. Cover and
microwave 4 minutes. Mince the meat or
chop finely in a food processor.
Mix the onion and cooking liquid with
the meat, rice, stock or water, tomato
purée, herbs and seasoning. Fill the pepper
cases with the mixture. Sprinkle on the
breadcrumbs. Cover and microwave 10
minutes. Remove the covering and
microwave 5 minutes.
Serve with gravy or with tomato sauce or
cheese sauce (see pages 78 and 76).

To freeze, cover with polythene or foil.
Storage life: 1 month. To serve, reheat in a
conventional oven at 190°C (375°F) mark 5
for 30 minutes or Defrost 5 minutes and
microwave 10 minutes.

PUDDINGS

Many types of pudding cook well in a
microwave oven, and the short cooking times
are a bonus to a busy cook.

A microwave oven is invaluable for preparing quick puddings. Fruit may be quickly cooked in water, cider or wine (although tough skins may not soften during the short cooking time); or baked apples may be prepared with a dried fruit or mincemeat filling, or with just sugar, butter and a little water; 4 apples will take only 6 minutes to cook depending on their size. Very little liquid is needed when cooking fruit by microwave, and the flavour of the finished dish will be strong and rich. For each 450 g (1 lb) fruit, 4 tablespoonfuls water will be enough (and rhubarb and cherries need only 2 tablespoonfuls). Berry fruits, including blackberries, do not need any water at all. The fruit is best placed in a casserole with the water and covered with clingfilm; leave the fruit to stand for a few minutes after microwaving and then sweeten to taste with sugar or honey, as fruit cooked in the microwave has a more intense flavour and it is difficult to assess how much sweetening will be needed before cooking.

Pastry can be cooked by microwave, and the flavour is good but the pastry remains very pale and looks unappetizing. It is better therefore to prepare pastry cases by conventional cooking (they may be frozen and kept ready for emergencies). A filling may then be added and the dish completed in the microwave oven so that speed is combined with an attractive appearance.

Steamed puddings, both of the sponge and suet variety, are particularly successful in a microwave oven, saving hours of steaming and a messy kitchen. They may be cooked very quickly and rise extremely well, so plenty of space must be left in the basin, which should be very lightly greased, or lined with clingfilm. At the end of the cooking time, a pudding may still look rather moist on top, but the pudding should be left to stand in the basin for 5 minutes before turning out, and it will then be cooked completely through. It is important to check with the manufacturer's booklet, because in some cookers, the 'Defrost' or 'Simmer' settings may be recommended for preparing these puddings. It is better not to put jam or syrup at the base of the pudding mixture as they become very hot in the oven and may burn before the rest of the pudding is cooked.

WINTER FRUIT COMPÔTE

Serves 4

450 g (1 lb) dried fruit
425 ml (¾ pint) China tea (without milk)
½ tsp ground mixed spice
150 ml (¼ pint) orange juice
2 oranges

Put the fruit (apricots, prunes, peaches, apples, pears) into a bowl and cover with the hot tea. Cover and microwave 12 minutes. Stir in the spice and orange juice and leave to stand for 30 minutes.

Peel the oranges and remove all the white pith. Cut the oranges across in slices and cut each slice in quarters. Stir into the bowl. Chill before serving with cream or natural yoghurt.

To freeze, pack into a freezer container. Storage life: 4 months. To serve, thaw at room temperature for 3 hours or Defrost 10 minutes and microwave 3 minutes.

PEARS IN RED WINE

Serves 4

8 eating pears
100 g (4 oz) caster sugar
150 ml (¼ pint) water
150 ml (¼ pint) red wine
5-cm (2-inch) cinnamon stick

Peel and core the pears and cut each one into 8 slices. Put the sugar and water into a bowl and microwave 2 minutes. Stir well and add the pears, wine and cinnamon. Cover and microwave 6 minutes.

Leave to stand until cool and then remove the cinnamon stick. Chill before serving with cream or natural yoghurt.

To freeze, pack into a freezer container. Storage life: 4 months. To serve, thaw at room temperature for 3 hours or Defrost 10 minutes and microwave 3 minutes.

GOLDEN PUDDING

Serves 4

150 g (5 oz) self-raising flour
pinch of salt
75 g (3 oz) butter or margarine
75 g (3 oz) caster sugar
2 eggs
4 tbsp milk
grated rind of 1 orange or 1 lemon

Sieve the flour and salt together. Cream the butter or margarine and sugar until light and fluffy. Beat the eggs and milk together. Add the flour and eggs alternately to the creamed mixture, beating well between each addition. Add the grated fruit rind and beat well.

Put into a greased 1.2-litre (2-pint) pudding basin and cover with clingfilm. Microwave 6 minutes. Leave to stand for 10 minutes. Turn out and serve with custard or sweet citrus sauce (see page 81).

To freeze, cool completely and leave in the basin. Cover with foil or polythene. Storage life: 2 months. To serve, cover with foil or greaseproof paper and steam for 1 hour (the pudding will toughen if microwaved again).

COTTAGE PUDDING

Serves 4

225 g (8 oz) self-raising flour
65 g (2½ oz) shredded suet
100 g (4 oz) soft light brown sugar
100 g (4 oz) seedless raisins
pinch of salt
6 tbsp milk
1 egg

Stir the suet and flour together and add the sugar, raisins and salt. Mix the milk and eggs and work into the flour. The mixture should be rather stiff. Put into a greased ovenware dish 20cm (8inches) square and microwave 8 minutes.

Serve sprinkled thickly with caster or demerara sugar and cut into wedges, with cream or custard as an accompaniment.

To freeze, cool completely and wrap in foil or polythene. Storage life: 2 months. To serve, reheat in a conventional oven at 190°C (375°F) mark 5 for 25 minutes (the pudding will toughen if microwaved again).

BROWN BREAD PUDDING

Serves 4

150 g (6 oz) brown breadcrumbs
275 ml (½ pint) milk
50 g (2 oz) seedless raisins
1 tsp ground cinnamon
pinch of ground nutmeg
pinch of salt
75 g (3 oz) butter
100 g (4 oz) soft light brown sugar
3 eggs

Put the breadcrumbs into a bowl. Pour the milk into a jug and microwave 3 minutes. Pour over the crumbs and stir in the raisins, cinnamon, nutmeg and salt. Cream the butter and sugar until light and fluffy and work in the eggs one at a time. Gradually work in the breadcrumb mixture to make a soft dough.

Grease a 1.2-litre (2-pint) pudding basin and put in the mixture. Loosely cover with clingfilm. Microwave 9 minutes. Leave to stand for 10 minutes.

Turn out and serve with cream or custard or warm golden syrup.

To freeze, cool completely and leave in the basin. Cover with foil or polythene. Storage life: 2 months. To serve, cover with foil or greaseproof paper and steam for 1 hour (the pudding will toughen if microwaved again).

RASPBERRY CRUMB PUDDING

Serves 4

450 g (1 lb) raspberries
100 g (4 oz) caster sugar
25 g (1 oz) butter
100 g (4 oz) fresh white breadcrumbs
3 eggs

Put the raspberries and sugar into a bowl and microwave 3 minutes, stirring twice. If frozen raspberries are used, Defrost for 4 minutes before adding sugar and microwaving on full power. Put through a sieve. Stir in the butter and pour over the breadcrumbs. Leave to stand for 30 minutes.

Beat the eggs and mix into the crumbs. Put into a deep 850-ml (1½-pint) ovenware dish and microwave 8 minutes. Leave until cold. Dust with icing sugar and serve.

To freeze, wrap in foil or polythene. Storage life: 2 months. To serve, thaw at room temperature for 3 hours or Defrost 5 minutes. Dust with icing sugar and serve.

DANISH APPLE PUDDING

Serves 4

700 g (1½ lb) eating apples
75 g (3 oz) fresh breadcrumbs
50 g (2 oz) soft light brown sugar
50 g (2 oz) butter
25 g (1 oz) drinking chocolate
    powder

Peel and core the apples and slice them thinly. Mix the breadcrumbs and sugar. Put the butter into a bowl and microwave 1 minute. Stir in the crumb mixture and microwave 2 minutes. Stir in the chocolate powder.

Arrange layers of apples and crumbs in a straight-sided 20-cm (8-inch) square ovenware dish, beginning with apples and ending with crumbs. Microwave 10 minutes. Serve hot or cold with cream.

To freeze, cool completely and wrap in foil or polythene. Storage life: 2 months. To serve cold, thaw at room temperature for 3 hours. To serve hot, reheat in a conventional oven at 190°C (375°F) mark 5 for 25 minutes or Defrost 5 minutes and microwave 5 minutes.

SPOTTED DICK

Serves 4

50 g (2 oz) self-raising flour
50 g (2 oz) brown breadcrumbs
50 g (2 oz) shredded suet
25 g (1 oz) soft light brown sugar
½ tsp ground mixed spice
75 g (3 oz) currants
1 egg
3 tbsp milk

Stir together the flour, breadcrumbs, suet and sugar with the spice until evenly coloured. Put the currants into a small bowl and cover with cold water. Microwave 2 minutes and drain well. Mix with the dry ingredients and beat in the egg and milk.

Grease an 850-ml (1½-pint) pudding basin and pour in the mixture. Cover with clingfilm and microwave 6 minutes. Leave to stand for 2 minutes and turn out. Place on a serving plate and serve with custard or warm golden syrup.

To freeze, cool completely and leave in the basin. Cover with foil or polythene and freeze. Storage life: 2 months. To serve, cover with foil or greaseproof paper and steam for 1 hour (the pudding will toughen if microwaved again).

BAKED CHEESECAKE

Serves 4

Base
100 g (4 oz) digestive biscuits
25 g (1 oz) caster sugar
25 g (1 oz) demerara sugar
½ tsp ground mixed spice
50 g (2 oz) butter

Filling
450 g (1 lb) cream cheese
100 g (4 oz) caster sugar
2 eggs
1 lemon
1 tbsp cornflour
50 g (2 oz) sultanas
275 ml (½ pint) soured cream

Crush the biscuits with a rolling pin or in a blender or food processor. Mix with the caster and demerara sugars and spice. Put the butter into a bowl and microwave 1 minute. Stir in the crumb mixture. Press the crumbs into the base of a 20-cm (8-inch) ovenware flan dish.

Put the cream cheese into a bowl and break it up with a fork. Add 75 g (3 oz) of the sugar and the eggs and beat until smooth and creamy. Grate the lemon rind and squeeze out the juice. Mix with the cornflour and beat into the cheese. Fold in the sultanas. Put on top of the crumb mixture and microwave 6 minutes. Mix the soured cream and remaining sugar and spread on top of the filling. Microwave 3 minutes. Spread the topping evenly again and microwave 3 minutes. Leave to cool.

To freeze, open-freeze and wrap in foil or polythene. Storage life: 1 month. To serve, thaw at room temperature for 3 hours or Defrost 5 minutes.

CHRISTMAS PUDDING

Makes two puddings; each serves 6–8

100 g (4 oz) plain flour
100 g (4 oz) fine brown breadcrumbs
100 g (4 oz) soft dark brown sugar
100 g (4 oz) softened butter
1 medium carrot
1 medium eating apple
2 tbsp black treacle
2 eggs
4 tbsp brandy or milk
1 tbsp lemon juice
1½ tsp ground mixed spice
½ tsp gravy browning
225 g (8 oz) seeded raisins
225 g (8 oz) sultanas
225 g (8 oz) currants
50 g (2 oz) chopped mixed peel
50 g (2 oz) glacé cherries, chopped

Stir together the flour and breadcrumbs. Cream the butter and sugar until light and fluffy. Work in the flour and breadcrumbs. Peel the carrot and apple and grate finely. Add to the mixture with all the remaining ingredients and beat well until thoroughly mixed. Grease two 1-litre (2-pint) pudding basins and fill with the mixture. Cover with a clean cloth and leave to stand overnight so that the flavours develop.

Cover with clingfilm and microwave each pudding 5 minutes. Leave to stand for 5 minutes, then microwave again for 5 minutes. Leave to stand for 10 minutes before turning out.

Turn onto a warm serving plate, flame with brandy and serve with cream, custard and/or brandy butter.

To freeze, leave in the basins, and cover with polythene. Storage life: 12 months. To serve, cover with foil or greaseproof paper and steam for 2 hours. In an emergency, if a pudding is needed quickly from the freezer, sprinkle with 2 tablespoonfuls water or brandy, cover with clingfilm and Defrost 15 minutes until hot.

FRUIT CRUMBLE

Serves 4

350 g (12 oz) fruit (rhubarb, apples,
  plums, gooseberries or
  blackcurrants)
75 g (3 oz) caster sugar
2 tbsp water
50 g (2 oz) butter
75 g (3 oz) demerara sugar
50 g (2 oz) wholemeal flour
50 g (2 oz) porridge oats
½ tsp baking powder
½ tsp ground mixed spice

Prepare the fruit and put into a deep 850-ml (1½-pint) dish with the caster sugar and water, and stir well (if using frozen fruit, thaw before preparing the dish). Cream the butter and work in the remaining ingredients to make a crumble topping. Sprinkle over the fruit and press down very lightly. Microwave 12 minutes. Leave to stand for 10 minutes as the fruit will be hot.

To serve, sprinkle with a little demerara sugar, or brown lightly under a hot grill if a golden finish is liked. Serve with cream.

To freeze, cool completely and wrap in foil or polythene. Storage life: 4 months. To serve, reheat in a conventional oven at 190°C (375°F) mark 5 for 45 minutes or Defrost 10 minutes and microwave 12 minutes before browning under a grill if liked, or sprinkling with demerara sugar.

RHUBARB AND GINGER FLAN

Serves 4

Base
75 g (3 oz) butter
175 g (6 oz) ginger biscuits

Filling
175 g (6 oz) chopped rhubarb
25 g (1 oz) butter
50 g (2 oz) sultanas
grated rind and juice of 1 lemon
3 tbsp soft light brown sugar
2 tbsp white breadcrumbs
1 egg
pinch of ground ginger

Prepare the base first. Crush the biscuits in a blender or food processor, or break them into crumbs with a rolling pin. Put the butter into a bowl and microwave 1 minute. Work in the crumbs and line the base and sides of an 18-cm (7-inch) flan dish.

To make the filling, put the butter into a bowl and microwave 20 seconds. Stir in the rhubarb and sultanas. Add the lemon rind and juice to the rhubarb. Stir in the sugar and breadcrumbs. Cover and microwave 6 minutes. Cool for 15 minutes and beat in the egg and ginger. Pour into the flan case and microwave 1½ minutes. Serve warm or cold with cream.

To freeze, cool completely and leave in the flan dish. Cover with foil or polythene and freeze. Storage life: 2 months. To serve, thaw at room temperature for 3 hours or Defrost 5 minutes and microwave 5 minutes to serve hot.

ALMOND CRUMB TART

Serves 4

Base
100 g (4 oz) plain flour
50 g (2 oz) butter
25 g (1 oz) caster sugar
2 egg yolks

Filling
50 g (2 oz) unsalted butter
50 g (2 oz) caster sugar
50 g (2 oz) spongecake crumbs
25 g (1 oz) ground almonds
1 egg
2 tsp lemon juice
almond essence
3 tbsp strawberry or apricot jam

Icing
100 g (4 oz) icing sugar
1 tbsp water

To make the pastry, sieve the flour and work in the butter, sugar and beaten egg yolks with the tips of the fingers. Wrap the pastry in foil and chill for 15 minutes. Roll out the pastry and line a 20-cm (8-inch) flan dish (the pastry is rather fragile so a little patching may be necessary to line the dish evenly). Prick lightly with a fork and microwave 6 minutes.

To make the filling, cream the butter and sugar until light and fluffy. Work in the cake crumbs, almonds, beaten egg, lemon juice and a few drops of almond essence. Cool the flan case for 5 minutes and then spread with jam to cover the base completely. Spread on the filling. Microwave 5 minutes. Leave until cold.

Mix the icing sugar and water and spread over the surface of the tart. Place on a serving dish and serve with cream or custard.

To freeze, do not ice; wrap in foil or polythene. Storage life: 4 months. To serve, thaw at room temperature or Defrost 10 minutes. Ice and serve with cream or custard.

SAVOURY AND SWEET SAUCES

This chapter includes some delicious and easy-to-make sauces to accompany the various recipes mentioned elsewhere in the book.

Sauces are extremely easy to make in the microwave oven, and it can be very useful to prepare them at the last minute before a meal without using space on a stove, and creating a lot of extra washing-up. A sauce may be prepared in a jug or sauceboat (a large quantity is best prepared in a basin to allow plenty of space for stirring). If a sauce has been prepared ahead by conventional means, it is also very easy to put it into a serving dish and reheat in the microwave, just stirring to mix well again.

Be careful to blend the liquid very thoroughly with the flour or cornflour used in the sauce, and to stir well two or three times during cooking. There is less evaporation when cooking by microwave, and sauces may be a little thinner than when cooked in a pan.

BROWN SAUCE

Makes 275 ml (½ pint)

1 small onion
1 small carrot
25 g (1 oz) butter
25 g (1 oz) plain flour
275 ml (½ pint) beef stock
salt and pepper

Chop the onion and carrot finely. Put the butter into a jug and microwave 30 seconds. Add the onion and carrot, cover and microwave 5 minutes. Mix in the flour and blend in the stock gradually. Microwave 3 minutes, stirring twice. Put through a sieve or blend in a liquidiser. Season to taste with salt and pepper. Microwave 30 seconds.

To serve, place in sauceboat. If the sauce is a little thick, stir in a little extra stock, or add extra flavour with a little dry sherry.

To freeze, cool completely and pack in a freezer container, leaving headspace. Storage life: 6 months. To serve, reheat in double saucepan or microwave 2 minutes; stir well and microwave 3 minutes, stirring twice.

WHITE SAUCE

Makes 275 ml (½ pint)

25 g (1 oz) butter
25 g (1 oz) plain flour
275 ml (½ pint) milk
salt and pepper

Put the butter into a jug. Microwave 30 seconds. Mix in the flour and gradually work in the milk. Microwave 3 minutes, stirring twice. Season with salt and pepper. Use hot with savoury dishes, or add flavourings (see Variations).

To freeze, cool completely and pack in a freezer container, leaving headspace. Storage life: 6 months. To serve, reheat in a double saucepan or microwave 2 minutes; stir well and microwave 3 minutes, stirring twice.

Variations
(1) Caper sauce: add 2 teaspoonfuls bottled capers when the sauce is cooked.
(2) Cheese sauce: add 75 g (3 oz) grated Cheddar cheese and a pinch of mustard powder.
(3) Egg sauce: add 1 finely-chopped hard-boiled egg.
(4) Parsley sauce: add 2 tablespoonfuls chopped fresh parsley.
(5) Prawn sauce: add 50 g (2 oz) peeled prawns and 1 teaspoonful lemon juice, and microwave 30 seconds.

ONION SAUCE

Makes 275 ml (½ pint)

1 large onion
25 g (1 oz) butter
25 g (1 oz) plain flour
275 ml (½ pint) milk
salt and pepper

Chop the onion very finely. Put the butter into a jug and microwave 30 seconds. Add the onion, cover and microwave 3 minutes, stirring twice. Mix in the flour and blend in the milk gradually. Microwave 3 minutes, stirring twice. Season to taste with salt and pepper. Place in a sauceboat and serve with lamb or steak.

To freeze, cool completely and pack in a
freezer container, leaving headspace.
Storage life: 6 months. To serve, reheat in a
double saucepan or microwave 2 minutes;
stir well and microwave 3 minutes, stirring
twice.

BREAD SAUCE

Makes 275 ml (½ pint)

1 small onion
6 cloves
275 ml (½ pint) milk
75 g (3 oz) fresh white breadcrumbs
25 g (1 oz) butter
2 tbsp double cream
salt and pepper

Peel the onion and stick the cloves into it.
Put into a bowl with the milk. Cover and
microwave 4 minutes. Discard the cloves
and chop the onion very finely. Return the
onion to the milk with the breadcrumbs and
butter. Microwave 2 minutes, stirring
twice. Stir in the cream, salt and pepper.
Microwave 30 seconds. Place in a sauceboat
and serve with poultry, game or sausages.

To freeze, cool completely and pack in a
freezer, leaving headspace. Storage life: 2
months. To serve, reheat in double
saucepan or microwave 2 minutes; stir well
and microwave 3 minutes, stirring twice.

BARBECUE SAUCE

Makes 275 ml (½ pint)

1 medium onion
25 g (1 oz) butter
1 garlic clove, crushed
15 g (½ oz) plain flour
1 tbsp Worcestershire sauce
1 tsp tabasco sauce
25 g (1 oz) soft dark brown sugar
1 tbsp vinegar
275 ml (½ pint) tomato juice
salt and pepper

Chop the onion very finely. Put into a bowl with the butter and garlic. Cover and microwave 3 minutes. Mix in the flour, and then all the remaining ingredients. Microwave 6 minutes, stirring three times. Place in a sauceboat and serve with steak, chops, chicken or sausages or brush onto meat which is to be grilled or barbecued.

To freeze, cool completely and pack in a freezer container, leaving headspace. Storage life: 2 months. To serve, reheat in a double saucepan or microwave 2 minutes; stir and microwave 3 minutes, stirring twice.

FRESH TOMATO SAUCE

Makes 275 ml (½ pint)

50 g (2 oz) bacon
25 g (1 oz) butter
1 small onion
1 small carrot
1 garlic clove
450 g (1 lb) fresh or canned tomatoes
25 g (1 oz) plain flour
275 ml (½ pint) water
1 bay leaf
1 tsp soft dark brown sugar
salt and pepper

Chop the bacon finely and put into a bowl with the butter. Cover and microwave 1 minute. Chop the onion, carrot and garlic finely and add to the bowl. Microwave 3 minutes. Chop the tomatoes and add to the bowl (reserve any juice from canned tomatoes). Cover and microwave 1 minute.

Mix the flour with a little of the water or reserved tomato juice, and then add enough water and/or reserved juice to make up to 275 ml (½ pint). Stir in the bay leaf and sugar. Cover and microwave 4 minutes, stirring twice. Put through a sieve and season to taste with salt and pepper. Microwave 1 minute.

To freeze, cool completely and pack in a freezer container, leaving headspace. Storage life: 2 months. To serve, reheat in a double saucepan or microwave 2 minutes; stir and microwave 3 minutes, stirring twice.

SPAGHETTI SAUCE

Makes 275 ml (½ pint)

1 medium onion
1 garlic clove, crushed
2 tbsp oil
450 g (1 lb) raw minced beef
450 g (1 lb) canned tomatoes
2 tbsp tomato purée
150 ml (¼ pint) beef stock
150 ml (¼ pint) red wine
½ tsp dried mixed herbs
salt and pepper

Chop the onion very finely. Put the oil into a large bowl, cover and microwave 1 minute. Add the onion and garlic, cover and microwave 3 minutes. Add the mince and break up well with a fork. Cover and microwave 2 minutes.

Chop the tomatoes roughly and add to the bowl with their juice, the tomato purée, beef stock, wine, herbs, salt and pepper. Stir well, cover and microwave 15 minutes, stirring three times. Leave to stand for 5 minutes. Pour over spaghetti or use to fill cannelloni or to make lasagne.

To freeze, cool completely and pack in a freezer container. Storage life: 2 months. To serve, reheat gently in a double saucepan or Defrost 5 minutes and microwave 6 minutes.

APPLE SAUCE

450 g (1 lb) cooking apples
5 tbsp water or dry cider
25 g (1 oz) sugar
25 g (1 oz) butter

Peel and core the apples and slice them thinly. Put into a bowl with the water or cider. Cover and microwave 3 minutes, stirring twice. Beat well with a wooden spoon and add the sugar and butter. Microwave 1 minute. Use hot or cold with pork, duck, goose or ham, or with sweet puddings.

To freeze, cool completely and pack in a freezer container, leaving headspace. Storage life: 12 months. To serve, thaw at room temperature for 1 hour or microwave 3 minutes and stir well.

RICH CHOCOLATE SAUCE

Makes 150 ml (¼ pint)

150 ml (¼ pint) water
100 g (4 oz) caster sugar
50 g (2 oz) cocoa

Put the water into a bowl and microwave 3 minutes. Stir in the sugar until dissolved and microwave 2 minutes. Add a little of the liquid to the cocoa powder to make a smooth paste. Add to the remaining hot liquid and microwave 1 minute. Leave to stand for 5 minutes, stirring occasionally. Use hot or cold with puddings or ices.

To freeze, cool completely and pack in a freezer container, leaving headspace. Storage life: 2 months. To serve, thaw at room temperature for 1 hour or microwave 3 minutes.

BUTTERSCOTCH SAUCE

Makes 150 ml (¼ pint)

225 g (8 oz) soft dark brown sugar
150 ml (¼ pint) single cream
40 g (1½ oz) butter
25 g (1 oz) chopped walnuts

Put the sugar in a bowl and stir in the cream. Cut the butter into thin flakes and stir into the bowl. Cover and microwave 4 minutes, stirring twice. Stir in the chopped nuts. Use hot or cold with puddings or ices.

To freeze, cool completely and pack in a freezer container, leaving headspace. Storage life: 2 months. To serve, thaw at room temperature for 1 hour or microwave 3 minutes.

SWEET CITRUS SAUCE

Makes 275 ml (½ pint)

275 ml (½ pint) orange juice
grated rind and juice of 1 lemon
15 g (½ oz) cornflour
25 g (1 oz) caster sugar

Reserve 2 tablespoonfuls orange juice and put the rest into a jug. Microwave 3 minutes. Mix the lemon juice with the cornflour, sugar and reserved orange juice. Add a little of the hot orange juice and mix well. Add to the remaining juice and microwave 3 minutes, stirring twice. Stir in the grated lemon rind and leave to stand for 5 minutes.

Stir well and serve hot on sweet puddings. If liked, a little orange liqueur may be stirred in after cooking.

To freeze, cool completely and pack in a freezer container, leaving headspace. Storage life: 2 months. To serve, thaw at room temperature for 1 hour and reheat in a double saucepan or microwave 3 minutes, stirring well.

CURRY SAUCE

Makes 275 ml (½ pint)

1 large onion
25 g (1 oz) butter
1 tbsp curry powder
1 tbsp plain flour
275 ml (½ pint) stock
2 tbsp mixed fruit chutney

Chop the onion very finely. Put the butter into a jug and microwave 30 seconds. Add the onion, cover and microwave 3 minutes, stirring twice. Mix in the curry powder and flour and add the stock gradually. Microwave 3 minutes, stirring twice. Stir in the chutney.

Serve with cooked chicken, eggs or vegetables.

To freeze: cool completely and pack in a freezer container, leaving headspace. Storage life: 2 months. To serve, reheat in a double saucepan or microwave 2 minutes, stir well and microwave 3 minutes, stirring twice.

CAKES

This chapter contains invaluable information to help you develop your skills of baking with a microwave oven.

It is not easy to bake cakes and biscuits in a microwave oven, but some recipes are very successful and microwaving is a very quick method of preparing them. Cakes rise well in the microwave oven, but they do not brown or gain an appetizing golden crust. Since microwave cakes do not take colour during baking, it is a good idea to use brown sugars, wheatmeal flour, chocolate or plenty of fruit to give natural colour to the finished product. When a naturally pale cake is baked, it needs to be finished with icing or a sprinkling of chopped nuts or with demerara sugar.

Choosing a recipe

Fatless sponges are not successful when baked by microwave. Scones and rock cakes which should have a crisp exterior, and which are not normally disguised by icing, are best avoided. Bread doughs are close and look unappetizing, although wholemeal bread can be passable, but the microwave oven is useful for proving doughs (see page 17). Biscuits are also difficult to prepare, as they do not brown and become very hard and dry.

The most successful cakes are fruit and chocolate, and those cakes which have plenty of texture given by wholemeal flour, coconut, ground nuts and demerara sugar. Tray-bakes with similar ingredients and with porridge oats are also good.

If you are adapting conventional recipes, a little extra liquid will be needed, as cakes dry quickly in the microwave oven. Milk rather than water will improve the keeping quality. Self-raising flour may be used, but if using plain flour and baking powder, reduce the raising agent by 25% as cakes rise more readily.

In an emergency, packet cake mixes may be used and these cook very well in the microwave oven.

Equipment

As with all microwave cooking, check the oven manufacturer's instructions before baking, to see if there are any special instructions for the individual cooker, and if variable controls can be used.

As in conventional baking, it is important to use the correct size of container, but this cannot be metal for microwaving. Special containers are obtainable, but everyday household utensils may be used. Straight-sided soufflé dishes or casseroles are very useful for deep cakes, while glass ovenware or ceramic flan dishes are fine for shallow ones. Oven-glass loaf dishes may be bought, and also ring moulds which give an excellent result as heat is distributed evenly (in a plain shaped mould, the centre of the cake takes a long time to cook and may become soggy). For small cakes, paper cases should be used, either standing on a plate, or with each individual case standing in an indentation in a microwave muffin dish.

Containers should not be greased and floured in the traditional way as this creates an unpleasant film on the outside of the cake. Some recipes advise light greasing, but normally the containers should be lined with greaseproof paper or clingfilm.

If a cake mixture is left to stand in the container for up to 10 minutes before baking, it will be very light and airy. For a deep cake, particularly fruit cake, stand the container on an upturned plate in the microwave cooker as this helps the centre of the cake to cook through. At the end of cooking time, microwave cakes look slightly soft and gooey, but cooking finishes when the cake is left to stand in its container. Do not be tempted to give the cakes a few extra minutes microwaving to finish cooking, or the result will be hard and rock-like. Leave the cake in the container until lukewarm before turning out.

Freezing and thawing
Microwave cakes may be frozen, although the reason for preparing them in a microwave cooker is usually that they are needed for immediate use. If cakes are iced, they should be open-frozen before packing. When a cake is needed from the freezer, it should be unwrapped and thawed at room temperature, but may be defrosted in the microwave oven for instant use. Iced cakes are best thawed naturally or the topping may be spoilt by the heat generated during the defrosting process.

CHOCOLATE CAKE

100 g (4 oz) demerara sugar
100 g (4 oz) butter
175 g (7 oz) self-raising flour
25 g (1 oz) drinking chocolate
*   powder*
1 large egg
5 tbsp milk

Butter cream
100 g (4 oz) icing sugar
50 g (2 oz) butter
1 tbsp cocoa, sifted
a little milk

Cream the sugar and butter until light and fluffy. Sieve the flour and drinking chocolate powder together. Beat the egg and milk lightly together. Add the flour and egg mixtures alternately to the creamed mixture. Beat well and place in an oiled 18-cm (7-inch) soufflé dish or microwave container. Microwave 6 minutes.

Cool in the dish and turn out. To make the butter cream, sift the icing sugar into a bowl. Add the butter and cream and beat together until smooth. Add the cocoa and a little milk if needed. Spread on top of the cake.

To freeze, wrap in foil or polythene. The cake may be frozen complete with butter icing, but in this case should be open-frozen before freezing. Storage life: 4 months. To serve, thaw at room temperature for 3 hours.

CHOCOLATE HAZELNUT CAKE

Base
100 g (4 oz) soft margarine
100 g (4 oz) caster sugar
2 eggs
100 g (4 oz) self-raising flour
50 g (2 oz) cocoa
50 g (2 oz) finely ground hazelnuts
150 ml (¼ pint) milk

Filling
50 g (2 oz) unsalted butter
50 g (2 oz) icing sugar
50 g (2 oz) finely ground hazelnuts

Icing
100 g (4 oz) plain chocolate
25 g (1 oz) butter

Cream the margarine and sugar until light and fluffy. Beat the eggs lightly together. Sieve the flour and cocoa together. Add the eggs and flour alternately to the creamed mixture, beating well between each addition. Fold in the hazelnuts. Stir in the milk and beat until the mixture is light and fluffy. Put into a 20-cm (8-inch) round dish lined with clingfilm. Microwave 7 minutes. Leave to stand for 15 minutes and turn onto a wire rack to cool.

When completely cold, split carefully and fill. Make the filling by creaming the butter until soft and working in the icing sugar and hazelnuts.

Finish the cake by making the topping. Put the chocolate and butter into a bowl and microwave 2 minutes. Stir well until smooth and pour over the cake. Leave until cold and place on a serving plate.

To freeze, put on a cakeboard and open-freeze before wrapping. Storage life: 4 months. To serve, thaw at room temperature for 3 hours.

BOILED FRUIT CAKE

225 g (8 oz) mixed dried fruit
100 g (4 oz) block margarine
225 ml (8 fl oz) strong tea (without milk)
100 g (4 oz) soft dark brown sugar
225 g (8 oz) self-raising flour
1 tsp bicarbonate of soda
1 tsp ground mixed spice
1 egg

Put the fruit into a bowl. Cut the margarine into small pieces and mix with the fruit. Pour on the tea. Microwave 4 minutes. Stir in the sugar and leave until cold. Sieve the flour with the soda and spice. Beat into the fruit mixture with the egg. Line a 20-cm (8-inch) round dish with clingfilm. Put in the mixture. Microwave 7 minutes.

Leave to stand for 15 minutes and turn on to a wire rack to cool. Leave until completely cold and put on a serving dish.

To freeze, pack in a polythene bag. Storage life: 4 months. To serve, thaw at room temperature for 3 hours.

CHERRY COCONUT CAKE

50 g (2 oz) desiccated coconut
4 tbsp milk
150 g (5 oz) soft margarine
150 g (5 oz) caster sugar
2 eggs
3 drops lemon essence
200 g (7 oz) self-raising flour
75 g (3 oz) glacé cherries

Icing
100 g (4 oz) icing sugar
1 tbsp lemon juice
25 g (1 oz) desiccated coconut

Put the coconut into a small bowl. Put the milk into a mug and microwave 20 seconds. Pour onto the coconut and leave to stand. Cream the margarine and sugar until light and fluffy. Beat the eggs with the lemon essence. Sieve the flour. Add eggs and flour alternately to the creamed mixture, beating well between each addition. Beat in the soaked coconut. Chop the cherries finely and fold into the mixture.

Line a 20-cm (8-inch) round dish with clingfilm. Put in the mixture. Microwave 6 minutes. Leave to stand for 15 minutes and turn onto a wire rack to cool. Mix the icing sugar and lemon juice and spread on the cake. Sprinkle with coconut. Place on a serving dish.

To freeze, pack in a polythene bag. Storage life: 4 months. To serve, thaw at room temperature for 3 hours.

CELEBRATION FRUIT CAKE

175 g (6 oz) butter
175 g (6 oz) soft dark brown sugar
2 tbsp black treacle
225 g (8 oz) wholemeal self-raising
flour
2 tsp ground mixed spice
3 eggs
2 tbsp milk
700 g (1½ lb) mixed dried fruit
100 g (4 oz) glacé cherries

Cream the butter, sugar and treacle until light and fluffy. Stir together the flour and spice. Beat the eggs and milk together lightly. Add the flour and eggs alternately to the creamed mixture, beating well between each addition. Fold in the dried fruit. Cut the cherries in quarters and fold into the mixture.

Line a 20-cm (8-inch) round dish with greaseproof paper. Put in the mixture. Microwave on Defrost for 45 minutes. Remove the cake from the oven and cover the top with a piece of foil. Leave to stand for 1 hour before turning onto a wire rack to cool. Leave until cold and place on a serving plate.

It is not necessary to freeze rich fruit cakes, and this one will keep well in a tin.

GOLDEN LEMON SPONGE

175 g (6 oz) butter
175 g (6 oz) soft light brown sugar
grated rind and juice of 1 lemon
175 g (6 oz) wholemeal self-raising
flour
pinch of salt
pinch of ground mixed spice
3 eggs

Icing
75 g (3 oz) butter
175 g (6 oz) icing sugar
juice of ½ lemon
1 tsp grated lemon rind

Cream the butter and sugar until light and fluffy. Beat the lemon rind into the butter. Mix the flour, salt and spice. Beat the eggs lightly. Add the flour and eggs alternately to the creamed mixture, beating well between each addition. Beat in the lemon juice.

Line a 20-cm (8-inch) ring mould with clingfilm and put in the mixture. Microwave 8 minutes. Leave to stand for 10 minutes and turn onto a wire rack to cool.

Cream the butter and icing sugar until light and fluffy and work in the lemon rind and juice. Spread all over the cake. Place on a serving plate. If liked, decorate with mimosa balls and angelica.

To freeze, do not decorate. Place on a cakeboard and open-freeze before wrapping in foil or polythene. Storage life: 4 months. To serve, thaw at room temperature for 3 hours.

CUP CAKES

Makes 12

50 g (2 oz) butter or margarine
50 g (2 oz) caster sugar
100 g (4 oz) self-raising flour
1 egg
3 tbsp milk
vanilla essence

Cream the butter or margarine and sugar. Sieve the flour. Beat the egg and milk together with a few drops of the essence. Add the egg mixture alternately to the creamed mixture, beating well between each addition. Divide between 12 individual paper cases. Place 6 cakes in a circle on a plate, or place in individual muffin moulds. Microwave 2 minutes. Cool on a wire rack. Repeat with the remaining cakes.

These cakes look very pale and should be finished with a little water icing and chopped nuts or a glacé cherry on each one.

To freeze, do not ice or decorate but pack in polythene. Storage life: 4 months. To serve, thaw at room temperature for 1 hour before icing and decorating.

Variations
(1) Chocolate buns: substitute 15 g (½ oz) cocoa powder for 15 g (½ oz) flour.
(2) Queen cakes: add 50 g (2 oz) mixed dried fruit.
(3) Orange or lemon cakes: substitute orange or lemon essence. Add ½ teaspoonful grated orange or lemon rind. Ice and decorate appropriately.
(4) Coffee buns: add 1 teaspoonful coffee essence instead of vanilla essence.

DATE LOAF

Makes one 900-g (2-lb) loaf

175 g (6 oz) soft dark brown sugar
50 g (2 oz) soft margarine
100 g (4 oz) plain flour
100 g (4 oz) plain wholemeal flour
pinch of salt
150 ml (½ pint) milk and water,
  mixed
1 tsp bicarbonate of soda
1 egg
100 g (4 oz) stoned dates

Cream the sugar and margarine until light and fluffy. Work in the flours and salt. Put the milk and water into a mug and microwave 2 minutes. Stir in the soda and add to the cake mixture. Add the egg and beat well. Fold in the finely chopped dates.

Grease a 900-g (2-lb) loaf dish and line the base with greaseproof paper. Put in the mixture and microwave 9 minutes. Leave to stand 10 minutes and turn onto a wire rack to cool. To serve, cut into slices and butter.

To freeze, wrap in foil or polythene. Storage life: 4 months. To serve, thaw at room temperature for 3 hours or Defrost 8 minutes. Cut into slices and butter.

CHOCOLATE OAT SQUARES

Makes 16

75 g (3 oz) butter
75 g (3 oz) golden syrup
100 g (4 oz) porridge oats
50 g (2 oz) sultanas
50 g (2 oz) chopped walnuts
25 g (1 oz) glacé cherries
100 g (4 oz) plain chocolate

Put the butter and syrup into a bowl and microwave 2 minutes. Stir in the oats, sultanas, walnuts and finely chopped cherries. Grease and base-line a 20-cm (8-inch) square dish. Spread in the oat mixture and microwave 5 minutes. Leave to stand for 15 minutes.

Break the chocolate into small pieces and put into a bowl. Microwave 2 minutes. Stir with a spoon until completely melted. Spread on top of the cake. Cool 15 minutes and mark into 16 squares. Finish cooling on a wire rack, then place on a serving dish.

To freeze, pack in a polythene bag. Storage life: 4 months. To serve, thaw at room temperature for 1 hour.

WALNUT BROWNIES

Makes 16

75 g (3 oz) plain chocolate
75 g (3 oz) butter or block margarine
175 g (6 oz) soft dark brown sugar
2 eggs
150 g (5 oz) plain flour
½ tsp baking powder
pinch of salt
2 tbsp milk
½ tsp vanilla essence
75 g (3 oz) chopped walnuts

Topping
100 g (4 oz) plain chocolate or 40 g
  (1½ oz) icing sugar

Break the chocolate into small pieces and put into a bowl with the butter or margarine. Microwave 2 minutes. Leave to stand for 5 minutes, stirring well until smooth and well mixed. Beat in the sugar and eggs. Sieve the flour with the baking powder and salt and beat into the chocolate mixture.

Mix the milk and vanilla essence and add to the cake mixture, beating well. Stir in the walnuts. Grease and base-line a 20-cm (8-inch) square dish. Put in the mixture and microwave 7 minutes. Leave to stand for 15 minutes. Mark into 16 squares and leave in the dish until cold. Lift the squares on to a wire rack.

Break up the chocolate and place in a bowl. Microwave 2 minutes. Beat with a spoon until smooth and spread on the surface of the brownie squares. If preferred, omit the chocolate and cover the surface with sieved icing sugar.

Leave until the topping chocolate has set and place on a serving plate.

To freeze, pack into a freezer container, but do not cover with chocolate or sugar. Storage life: 4 months. To serve, thaw at room temperature for 1 hour or Defrost 3 minutes. Cover with chocolate or icing sugar before serving.

NUTTY CHOCOLATE FINGERS

Makes 12

50 g (2 oz) hard margarine or butter
15 g (½ oz) caster sugar
75 g (3 oz) plain flour
1 egg yolk
1 tbsp water
1 tsp coffee powder

Topping
175 g (6 oz) plain chocolate
50 g (1½ oz) butter
50 g (2 oz) soft dark brown sugar
1 egg
1 tsp coffee powder
100 g (4 oz) chopped nuts

Cream the margarine or butter and sugar until light and fluffy. Work in the flour, egg yolk, water and coffee powder. Grease and base-line a 20-cm (8-inch) square dish. Spread the mixture in the base and microwave 2 minutes. Chop the chocolate finely and sprinkle on the surface of the cake. Microwave 1 minute. Spread the chocolate evenly over the cake and leave to stand for 10 minutes.

Put the butter into a bowl and microwave 30 seconds. Stir in the sugar, beaten egg, coffee powder and nuts. Spread over the chocolate. Microwave 6 minutes. Leave to stand 15 minutes and mark into 12 fingers. Cool in the dish. To serve, cut out fingers carefully and lift onto a serving plate.

To freeze, pack the fingers into a freezer container. Storage life: 4 months. To serve, thaw at room temperature for 1 hour or Defrost 3 minutes.

OAT CRUMBLES

Makes 16

175 g (6 oz) soft margarine
175 g (6 oz) soft dark brown sugar
200 g (7 oz) plain flour
½ tsp baking powder
½ tsp salt
175 g (6 oz) porridge oats
almond essence
100 g (4 oz) apricot or raspberry jam

Cream the margarine and sugar together until soft and fluffy. Sieve the flour, baking powder and salt together. Mix into the creamed mixture with the oats and a few drops of almond essence until well blended.

Grease and base-line a 20-cm (8-inch) square dish. Put in half the mixture and press down firmly with a fork. Put the jam into a bowl and microwave 30 seconds. Spread over the base. Put on the remaining cake mixture and press down lightly. Microwave 7 minutes. Leave to stand for 5 minutes and mark into 16 squares. Cool.

To serve, lift out of the baking dish carefully and arrange on a serving plate. If liked, sprinkle with sieved icing sugar.

To freeze, pack into a freezer container. Storage life: 4 months. To serve, thaw at room temperature for 1 hour or Defrost 3 minutes. If liked, sprinkle with icing sugar before serving.

APPLE AND LEMON CAKE

175 g (6 oz) unsalted butter
100 g (4 oz) caster sugar
3 eggs
grated rind and juice of 1 lemon
2 tbsp golden syrup
175 g (6 oz) self-raising flour
50 g (2 oz) chopped walnuts
1 eating apple

Icing
50 g (2 oz) unsalted butter
2 tbsp milk
200 g (7 oz) icing sugar
juice of ½ lemon

Cream the butter and sugar until light and fluffy. Beat the eggs together and gradually beat into the creamed mixture. Add the lemon rind and juice to the creamed mixture with the syrup. Fold in the flour and nuts.

Peel and core the apple and chop the flesh finely. Fold into the cake mixture. Line a 20-cm (8-inch) round dish with clingfilm. Spoon in the mixture. Microwave 5 minutes. Leave to stand 15 minutes and turn onto a wire rack to cool.

To make the icing, put the butter and milk into a bowl and microwave 30 seconds. Beat in the icing sugar and lemon juice. Cover the top of the cake. If liked, decorate with halved walnuts. Place on serving dish.

To freeze, place on a board and open-freeze. Pack in a polythene bag or foil. Storage life: 4 months. To serve, thaw at room temperature for 3 hours.

WHAT IS THE WI?

If you have enjoyed this book, the chances are that you would enjoy belonging to the largest women's organisation in the country — the Women's Institutes.

We are friendly, go-ahead, like-minded women, who derive enormous satisfaction from all the movement has to offer. This list is long — you can make new friends, have fun and companionship, visit new places, develop new skills, take part in community services, fight local campaigns, become a WI market producer, and play an active role in an organisation which has a national voice.

The WI is the only women's organisation in the country which owns an adult education establishment. At Denman College, you can take a course in anything from car maintenance to paper sculpture, from bookbinding to yoga, or cordon bleu cookery to fly-fishing.

All you need to do to join is write to us here at the **National Federation of Women's Institutes, 39 Eccleston Street, London SW1W 9NT**, or telephone 01-730 7212, and we will put you in touch with WIs in your immediate locality. We hope to hear from you.

ABOUT THE AUTHOR

Mary Norwak has written over 70 books, including *The Farmhouse Kitchen*, *English Puddings* and more than a dozen titles on freezer cookery. She gives cookery demonstrations to many different groups. A member of the WI for over 25 years, Mary Norwak belongs to Cley WI and serves on the Executive Committee of the Norfolk Federation of Women's Institutes.

INDEX